Have you ever awakened and wondered what your dream was all about? It was like a Hollywood movie - and you starred in it. Maybe you were about to step on to a bridge, or walking in slow motion on the day of an important test at school; or worse - standing naked in front of a crowd. This easy-to-use guide gives you a detailed list of dream pictures and feelings, and what they all mean.

Eili Goldberg has a Master's degree in the Humanities, and has published nine books on mysticism and psychology. He resides in Israel.

LITTLE **BIG** BOOK

SERIES:

LITTLE **BIG** BOOK

of

Dream
Interpretation

by Eili Goldberg

Astrolog Publishing House

Astrolog Publishing House
P.O. Box 1123, Hod Hasharon 45111, Israel
Tel./Fax: 972-9-7412044
E-Mail: info@astrolog.co.il
Astrolog Web Site: www.astrolog.co.il

ISBN 965-494-047-7

Published by Astrolog Publishing House 1998

Distribution:
U.S.A. & CANADA by APG -
Associated Publishers Group
U.K. & EUROPE by DEEP BOOKS
EAST ASIA by CKK Ltd.

Printed in Israel
10 9 8 7 6 5 4 3 2 1

The most fascinating thing about dreams is their interpretation. We all dream, and we all want to understand our dreams. This book is a complete lexicon of dreams aimed at helping us interpret our dreams and understand their meaning.

The entries are arranged alphabetically, and are based on both Eastern and Western cultural heritages.

We have also included newer ways of understanding dreams - those developed over the past century by various psychologists and psychiatrists, such as Freud and Jung.

It is up to you, the reader, to take this book... and fall asleep! Your dreams will unfold on their own — as will their meanings.

You may rest assured that you will be able to interpret your next dream! We have compiled a comprehensive lexicon of dreams which can help you interpret your dreams on your own.

A

Abandonment — If the dreamer is abandoned, this signifies a quarrel with a friend. If he abandons another person, it means that he will renew a contact with a friend.

Abundance — This is a clear indication that the dreamer will have a life filled with prosperity and wealth.

Abyss — Looking down into an abyss is a sign that the dreamer is about to encounter danger.

Accident — A traffic accident signifies that a bad decision will lead to an unsuccessful deal. If one dreams about an accident occurring in an unknown place, it indicates an unsuccessful love life. Dreaming about being involved in a railroad accident is an indication of exaggerated self-confidence. If the dreamer is in a plane crash, it is a warning against bad business deals in the near future.

Accordion — When the dreamer is playing the accordion, it is a sign that he will soon marry. If the sound of the instrument can only be heard and not seen, disappointment can be expected. Off-key music or notes indicate depression and despondency.

Accountant — Dreaming about an accountant is connected to the dreamer's financial problems. A conversation with an accountant means that the dreamer has a strong desire to raise his standard of living.

Acrobat — This signifies that the dreamer has a dangerous enemy of whom he is not aware. If an acrobat falls in the dream, it indicates that a plot has been foiled. If the dreamer himself is the acrobat, it means that he needs reinforcement from his surroundings.

 Actor — An actor on the stage indicates two-faced behavior on the part of one of the dreamer's friends.

 Adam and Eve — Such a dream signifies a person seeking the virginal or primal aspect of life, or an individual who lives a full life, in harmony with himself.

 Adultery — Indicates a guilty conscience regarding the dreamer's sexuality.

Age — If the dreamer himself or others close to him appear older than they are in reality, or if in the dream the dreamer is worried about his age, it means that he will become ill in the near future. If the dreamer or others close to him appear younger than in reality, it is advisable for the dreamer to avoid coming into conflict with those around him.

Agreement — This suggests that the dreamer's problems will be solved and his worries will disappear completely.

Albatross — The dreamer will overcome obstacles and reach his desired objective.

Alcoholic Beverages — If the dreamer is drinking alcoholic beverages, it means that he must beware of being misled.

Almonds — Eating almonds predicts a journey to distant places.

Amusement — Being amused or in a good mood in a dream means that the dreamer will soon have good luck. Dreaming about some kind of entertainment means that an opportunity is about to present itself, and it would be a shame to miss it.

Anchor — This symbolizes stability, security and earthiness. The dreamer has both feet firmly planted on the ground.

Angel — This is an indication of the dreamer's strong belief in a superior power; he makes no attempt to alter his own destiny. It also signifies a successful marriage.

Anger — This portends good and significant news for the dreamer. Anger at a person known to the dreamer indicates that the person does not deserve the dreamer's trust. Anger at an unknown person indicates that the dreamer's life will soon change for the better.

Animals — The meaning changes according to the type of animal. (Refer to the name of the particular animal.)

Animal Young/Cubs — If animal young appear with their mother in a dream, it indicates maternal feelings. Wild animal cubs symbolize a longing for happiness.

Domesticated animal young are indicative of the dreamer's childish personality.

Ankle — If the dreamer's ankle appears in the dream, it means success and the solving of problems. If his spouse's ankle appears, it indicates that the dreamer is being unfaithful to her, or the opposite.

Annoyance — If the dreamer expresses annoyance or anger, it is a sign that his life will be happy and successful.

Ants — A dream about ants suggests that the dreamer reorganize his professional life and make changes in it. Ants that are particularly tiresome indicate an imminent period of frustration and disappointment.

Appetite — A large appetite for food and drink is a sign of great sexual passion.

Apple — Eating an apple in a dream predicts a rosy future. If the apple is sour, it is a sign that the dreamer will soon be disappointed or experience failure.

Apricot — Dreaming about apricots or about eating them indicates a good future and success in most areas of life, with the exception of romance.

Arm — A strong arm signifies unexpected success. A weak arm means a great disappointment in the life of the dreamer.

Artichoke — This suggests faulty communication with one's partner, as well as disagreements and the lack of ability to understand him/her.

Artist — Dreams about artists, painters or other creative people actually indicate the contrary: the dreamer does not have artistic talent and would do better to pursue other avenues of development.

 Asparagus — This signifies correct and good decisions made by the dreamer. He should continue to follow his heart and not listen to the advice of others.

 Astronomer/Astrologer — This shows that the dreamer is facing the future with hope and positive expectations.

Auction — If a man dreams about an auction, it is a sign

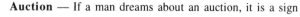

that his business will flourish. If a woman dreams about an auction, it means that she will be wealthy and live a life of affluence.

Aura — If the aura encircles the dreamer himself, it is a warning of a threat to his status and image.

Avalanche — If the dreamer is caught in an avalanche, it means good things are coming his way. If other people are caught in an avalanche, it is a sign that the dreamer is longing to move to a different place.

Avenue — An avenue of trees symbolizes ideal love. An avenue of trees shedding their leaves signifies a difficult life full of obstacles.

Avocado — This signifies economic success and an improvement in the dreamer's status in the work place.

Ax — An ax signifies the end of a family feud, fight or struggle. A sharp ax symbolizes progress; a blunt ax means that business will become slow.

B

Baby — Dreaming about an especially happy baby indicates that the dreamer will enjoy true love. Dreaming about a pretty baby predicts true friendship. Dreaming about a sick baby is a sign that the dreamer has treacherous friends.

Bachelorhood — If a married person dreams about bachelorhood, it indicates a secret wish to be unfaithful to his/her spouse.

Back Door — If the dreamer sees himself entering and leaving through a back door, it indicates an urgent need to effect changes in his life. If he sees another person leaving though the back door, he can expect a financial loss, and it is not advisable to enter into a business partnership.

Badger — This indicates the fear that someone else is harvesting the fruits of the dreamer's labors.

Bag/Handbag — This predicts the advent of good tidings and significant news concerning the dreamer's future.

Baker/Cook — This suggests that the dreamer does not have a clear conscience or is involved in some kind of scam; it reveals a desire to conceal a situation into which the dreamer is being coerced.

Ball (game) — If the dreamer is playing ball, it is a sign that he will soon receive good news. If the dreamer sees other people playing ball, it is a sign that he harbors an unhealthy jealousy toward one of his friends.

Ball (dance) — Participating in a ball indicates that the dreamer will have a happy and joyous life, full of love.

Ballet — This signifies betrayal, envy and quarrels.

Balloon — This indicates severe disappointments in the future. A large-than-usual balloon suggests ambitiousness. A balloon plunging from high above signifies regression.

Bananas — Bananas suggest that the dreamer is bored at work and is not exploiting his talents. Dreaming about eating a banana indicates a health problem.

Bandage — Wearing a bandage is a sign that the dreamer has loyal friends on whom he may depend.

Banking — Dreaming about being in a bank indicates business problems. If the dreamer meets the bank manager, it hints at bankruptcy. Money bills in a dream mean financial prosperity.

Banquet/Feast— Dreaming about a banquet with many participants predicts a quarrel with one's partner. If the dreamer is single, it indicates marriage in the near future, but one that will end in failure.

Bar (for drinking) — This indicates insecurity and a yearning for a better future. A bar with a bartender signifies that the dreamer is longing to throw a party.

Barbecue — This signifies that the dreamer is under extreme emotional pressure and is doing nothing to change the situation.

Barbershop/Beauty Parlor — If the dreamer is getting

his hair cut, it means that he is an ambitious person. The dream is also indicative of a strong character and a person who enjoys standing up for his rights and principles.

Barefoot — If the dreamer is barefoot, it is a sign that his path will be fraught with obstacles, but he will overcome them all.

Basket (woven) — An overflowing, woven straw basket is a sign of social and financial success. An empty basket, however, symbolizes disappointment, sadness and depression.

Bath — Dreaming about taking a bath indicates success in business. If the water is not clear, there might be problems and difficulties in the near future.

Bat (animal) — This is a warning about the advent of bad news.

Beach/Shore — This means that the dreamer needs some peace and quiet, some respite from the intensive life he leads.

Bear — When a bear appears in a dream, the dreamer will have to work hard before he sees the fruits of his labor. Killing a bear symbolizes overcoming obstacles on the path to attaining a certain goal.

Beard — A beard in a dream attests to the fact that the dreamer has a strong character and plenty of self-confidence (particularly a white beard).

Bed — Almost any situation in which a bed is seen in a dream predicts good things. Making the dreamer's bed indicates marriage in the near future. Making a stranger's bed symbolizes a new and surprising turning-point in life. An unmade bed indicates that the dreamer has problems with sexuality and marriage.

Bed-Linen/Sheets — Clean bed-linen means that the dreamer will soon receive good news from far away. Dirty bed-linen indicates financial losses or health problems.

Bedroom — This is usually connected to eroticism and sex. At times, it speaks of a positive turning-point in life.

Bee — A bee or bees in a dream signify that a joyous

occasion is soon to take place in the family. It also means that the dreamer has good friends.

Beehive — This indicates a wedding, birth or engagement in the near future.

Beetle — The dreamer can expect a brilliant future. He will become important and famous.

Beggar — If the dreamer helps a beggar, it means that he should expect good things in all areas of life. If the dreamer refuses to help the beggar, a loss is predicted.

Bell — The ringing of a bell in a dream portends bad news concerning a distant acquaintance.

Belt — The dreamer will soon receive a large sum of money unexpectedly.

Bicycle — This indicates a frenzied lifestyle and the need to slow down. Riding downhill warns of danger in the near future. Riding uphill signifies a rosy future.

Billiards — A billiard table with people around it indicates unexpected problems. An isolated pool table indicates that the dreamer should beware of those conspiring against him.

Bills — If the dreamer himself is paying bills, it is a sign that his financial concerns will disappear shortly without a trace. Worrying about not having paid bills means that the dreamer's enemies are spreading malicious gossip about him.

Billy-Goat — This is the symbol of a demon, the devil or an evil spirit.

Birds — If a rich man dreams of birds in flight, it is a sign that he will suffer financial losses. If a poor man or one with financial problems dreams of birds, it is a sign of economic abundance. A wounded bird means that a member of the dreamer's family will cause him harm.

Bird's Nest — An empty bird's nest predicts problems. A nest containing eggs indicates a rosy future.

Birth (of animals) — This indicates that the dreamer has enemies who are acting behind his back; however, he will overcome this obstacle and succeed in attaining his goals and objectives.

Birth (of people) — If a single person dreams about birth, it signifies that certain problems will soon be solved. If a married person dreams about birth, it is a sign that he will soon get pleasant surprises.

Biscuit/Cookie — This indicates that the dreamer has the tendency to blame others for his own mistakes and deeds.

Blackberries — These warn of financial disappointment or loss of economic status.

Blacksmith — It is quite rare to dream about a blacksmith. However, it indicates a spirit torn in two.

Blame — If the dreamer is being blamed for something, it suggests that he will be involved in a quarrel in the future. If the dreamer blames someone else, it means that he will quarrel with his associates.

Blanket — This indicates good times and a happy life: the thicker and more elaborately decorated the blanket, the happier the dreamer's life will be.

Blaze — Flames or a blaze indicate the eruption of bottled-up rage. Overcoming a blaze means that the dreamer will soon receive unexpected good news.

Bleeding — This warns of health problems which must be attended to.

Blindfold — A blindfold suggests that the dreamer was greatly disappointed by himself and by those around him.

Blindness — If the dreamer appears blind in a dream, he is not totally satisfied with his choice of a spouse. If he dreams about leading someone who is blind, it is a sign that he is too dependent on someone who does not actually deserve his trust.

Blood — This indicates an unwanted relationship, a quarrel, anger, disagreements or disappointment (particularly in emotional contexts).

Boat — This heralds changes for the better in the dreamer's life. A boat on calm waters indicates a change in work place or residence. Rowing a boat is a sign of social success as well as recognition from professional colleagues. If a boat overturns, it is a sign that the dreamer will soon receive important news. A boat on land means significant financial losses.

Book — Dreaming about a book signifies great success connected with reading or studying, which will lead the dreamer to a fulfilling and financially rewarding profession. Reading a book in a dream means that the dreamer will go on a trip which will have great significance in his life.

Bouquet (of flowers) — This indicates that the dreamer feels that his talents are not appreciated.

Bow and Arrow — The dreamer is aware of his talents and has great self-esteem. He knows how to rely on himself and his powers of judgment.

Bowl — A full bowl predicts quarrels or disagreements with a partner. An empty bowl is a sign of tranquillity, quiet and rest.

Box/Chest — A closed box means financial problems. An open box signifies that a secret, which the dreamer has jealously guarded until now, is about to be revealed. A box that has been broken into indicates licentiousness. A sealed box is a sign of morality.

Bracelet — Wearing a bracelet on one's wrist predicts marriage in the near future.

Bread — This signifies that the dreamer is satisfied with himself and derives pleasure from his family. Eating bread predicts good health.

Breakage — Any kind of breakage in a dream — no matter who is doing the breaking — portends bad things, mainly health problems.

Breakfast — This indicates that the individual is going to face a difficult test, and that he fears failure.

Bride — This is an indication of virginity, and a lack of maturity and experience of life.

Bridge — Crossing a bridge indicates exaggerated

concerns which will soon pass. A bridge which collapses is a warning of economic problems. An endless bridge signifies unrequited love. Passing underneath a bridge means that the dreamer must be patient if he is ever to solve his problems.

Broom — If the dreamer is sweeping with a broom, it indicates a professional turning point. A broom lying on the ground portends imminent separation from a close friend.

Brother/Sister — A dream about a sibling must be interpreted according to the character traits of the dreamer's family.

Building — If the dreamer is standing next to a luxurious building, it predicts good and pleasant times. If the dreamer enters the building, it means a loss of control, as well as nervousness and impatience.

Bull — If a woman dreams about a bull, it is a sign that she is not sexually satisfied. If a man dreams about a bull, it means he relates brutally to women.

Bundle — This warns the dreamer of a great disappointment in the near future.

Burglary — Dreaming about a break-in or burglary means that someone whom the dreamer has trusted implicitly is not worthy of such trust.

Burial — Contrary to what it seems, burial predicts birth or marriage.

Burn — If the dreamer gets burnt, it means he will soon win a large sum of money. If he sees another person getting burnt, it means he will soon make a new friend.

Butter — Dreaming about butter means that the dreamer is not focused, and instead of concentrating his efforts in one field, he spreads himself thinly over too many areas and does not succeed in any.

Butterfly — This indicates that the dreamer is involved in a passionate love affair.

Buttons — Wooden buttons predict success following considerable effort. Pearl buttons foretell a trip in the near future. Fabric buttons indicate that the dreamer's health is deteriorating and he must look after himself. Losing buttons in a dream signifies family problems as a result of financial losses. Finding a button in a dream signifies a promotion at work and prosperity in business.

C

Cabbage — This attests to the dreamer's lazy nature, a characteristic which significantly influences the achievements in his life.

Cage — If a single woman dreams about a cage, it is a sign that she will soon receive a proposal of marriage. If a man dreams about a cage, it means that he will get married prematurely. Two birds in a cage indicate a wonderful and happy married life.

Cake — Dreaming about a cake, particularly a festively decorated cake, indicates good health and happiness.

Calendar — This warns the dreamer that he underestimates important issues and disparages other people, and this may very likely have a boomerang effect.

Calling by name — When the dreamer is called by name or calls another by name, it is a sign that he will soon enter a good period regarding romance and marriage.

Camel — This portends a good future. The dreamer will overcome obstacles with the help of good friends.

Camping — Dreaming about sleeping outdoors warns against routine and signifies the need for a vacation. Dreaming about going to an army camp predicts marriage in the near future.

Canal — Dreaming about a canal of murky water is an indication of problems and worries. Clear water in a canal signifies that problems will soon be solved. Weeds growing in a canal warn of financial embroilment. Falling into a canal indicates a drop in status. Jumping over a canal means the dreamer will maintain his self-respect.

Candlesticks — A good sign: changes for the better in one's life, or participation in happy occasions and financial success.

Candy/Sweets — A box full of candy predicts that the dreamer's economic situation is about to improve. If a woman dreams of receiving a box of candies, it is a sign that she has a secret admirer. If the dreamer sends a box of candy to another person, it predicts a disappointment.

Cannibal — This is an indication of pressure, anxiety, or fears plaguing the dreamer. It is also possible that the dreamer is not physically healthy.

Cannibalism — This indicates a tendency toward self-destruction and loss of self-control.

Cannon — This predicts war, conflict or quarrels.

Cape — If the dreamer is wearing a cape, it is a sign that he inspires a feeling of confidence in his friends. If another person is wearing a cape, it is a sign that the dreamer deems him highly trustworthy.

Captain — Dreaming about a captain (of a boat or airplane) attests to the dreamer's ambitious nature and his desire to rule and lead others.

Car — Any kind of dream about a car means good things: problems will be solved, complications will sort themselves out and life will flow smoothly.

Caravan — This indicates that the dreamer will embark on a journey in the near future, and that he must beware of physical harm.

Cards — Winning a card game is a prediction of marriage in the near future. Losing a card game signifies that the dreamer will soon be forced to take risks.

Carpentry — This signifies that the dreamer is bored with his profession or occupation and needs variety.

Carpet — Walking on a carpet indicates a love of luxury. Cleaning a carpet means personal problems in one's domestic or romantic life.

Carrot — This signifies that the dreamer is not coping with his problems and chooses to ignore them.

Cat — This is an indication of cunning, subversion, lack of trust and treachery. The dream urges the dreamer to examine his friends and confidants carefully.

Cattle — This indicates financial success in the near future. It attests to the dreamer's conservative personality and tendency to calculate his every step.

Cauliflower — The dreamer can expect quiet times and a calm period in his life.

Cave — If the dreamer is hiding in a cave, it is a sign that someone is spreading vicious rumors about him and wishes to cause him harm.

Celebration/Party — If the dreamer is enjoying a celebration or party, it is a sign of good things to come. A dream of a formal party — without dancing or warmth — is a sign that the dreamer has made several mistakes for which he must now pay the price.

Celery — This means that only good things will come the way of the dreamer, bringing abundance, happiness and joy into his life.

Cellar — This indicates a loss of the dreamer's self-confidence. Dreaming about a wine-cellar represents a warning against marrying a gambler.

Cement — Any form of cement in a dream means a change for the better or an improvement in the dreamer's financial status.

Cemetery — This indicates that good news is on the way, or that a sick friend is recovering. A dream of the death of a family member predicts a period of stress and problems.

Cereal/Porridge — This warns of dangerous enemies that may embroil the dreamer.

Chain — A good sign. Wearing a gold or silver chain predicts that the dreamer will receive a gift from an admirer or lover. Dreaming about the clasp of a chain indicates that the dreamer's problems will soon be solved.

Chair — If someone is sitting on the chair, it heralds the arrival of another person bringing money. An empty chair signifies that the dreamer is about to receive news from a friend abroad.

Champion/Championship — This indicates that the dreamer is ambitious and competitive, and will do anything to attain his goals.

Charity — Receiving charity is a sign that the dreamer's financial status will deteriorate slightly, but not significantly. Giving charity in a dream is a sign of improvement in his financial status.

Cheese (hard, yellow) — This indicates that the dreamer has a difficult character and an uncompromising stubbornness that alienates his friends.

Cherries — These represent good-naturedness and loyalty and predict good things. Eating cherries is a sign that one's wishes are about to come true.

Chess — If the dreamer is playing chess, he can expect to have a serious quarrel with a friend or relative, with bitter consequences. A chessboard means that the dreamer will meet new people as a result of a crisis which he has undergone.

Chest (body) — Whether it is a man's or a woman's chest, it is a symbol of an intimate relationship with a person who is close.

Chick — For those involved in agriculture and breeding chickens, this predicts damage. For others, it indicates that they count their chickens before they're hatched, and should be more realistic.

Children — If a woman dreams about children, it means that she is satisfied with her family life. If a man dreams about children, it means that he can expect a period of quiet with regard to his domestic life.

Chiming of a Clock — This image always heralds good things: the louder the chiming, the happier life will be.

Chimney — This predicts success. A smoking chimney

heralds good tidings coming the way of the dreamer. A broken chimney is a foreboding of worries and problems.

Chrysanthemum — This usually symbolizes love or deep affection.

Cigarettes — If someone lights a cigarette for the dreamer, it means that the latter will soon need assistance from another person. If a cigarette butt appears in an ashtray, it indicates the inability to fulfill hopes and desires.

Cleanliness — A dream about the cleanliness of objects means that the dreamer will soon have to shoulder an unbearable burden and experience feelings of extreme oppression.

Climb — Any type of climb - up a mountain, a ladder, etc. - means that the dreamer will overcome all the obstacles that stand in the way of attaining his objectives.

Clock — Any sort of clock attests to the dreamer's achievement-oriented character, or to his actual achievements; it also symbolizes wealth and abundance.

Clothing — A closet full of clothing means that the dreamer can soon expect problems in different areas. If he is partially dressed, he is able to attain his objective. Getting dressed in a dream means progress. Getting undressed means regression. If the dreamer is dressed eccentrically, it indicates substantial success.

Clover — Because of the shape of its leaves, clover symbolizes a fork in the dreamer's path.

Clown — This shows that the dreamer is living a dishonest and deceitful life. Masks mean that one is two-faced.

 Coat — Almost any context in which a coat appears (worn, sold or bought) indicates that a certain investment will pay off and the dreamer will benefit from it. Wearing a coat that belongs to someone else means that the dreamer needs help from that person. Losing a coat in a dream indicates that the dreamer should be cautious when making any business decisions.

Cobra — This is a sign of serious sexual problems (particularly in the case of men).

Coffee — This means that the dreamer is under emotional pressure and suffers from tension in his daily life.

Coins — A gold coin indicates that the dreamer has gone out to enjoy nature. A worn coin predicts a dreary day. A copper coin means a heavy burden and serious responsibility. A shining coin means success in romance.

Collar — If the collar is tight around the dreamer's neck, it signifies that he is afraid of a strong person who intimidates him.

Colors — All the colors of the spectrum, except black, are a good sign. Bright colors - security and tranquillity; white - innocence and purity; blue - overcoming problems with the help of one's friends; yellow - high expectations; orange or gray - one must have patience; red - social events; green - envy; brown - good news; pink - a surprise; black - bad moods and depression.

Comb — If the dreamer is combing his hair, it means that a sick friend needs his help.

Compass — This symbolizes loyalty: the dreamer has loyal friends who will come to his aid in times of trouble.

Conference (business) — This means that the dreamer's financial situation will improve.

Confusion — Chaos and disorder in a dream warn of accidents and obstacles. One should be more alert.

Contest/Competition — This means that the dreamer must resist strong temptation.

Conversation — A conversation between the dreamer and another person indicates difficulties that may arise at work or in business, such as theft, damage, etc.

Cooking — This is usually connected with sexuality. The different stages of cooking — before, during and after — are parallel to the past, present and future in the dreamer's life. Dreaming about cooking also warns of health problems.

Coral — This warns against taking a particular step in any area of life.

Corpse — This indicates that the dreamer is dealing with death, the occult or infinity. If a businessman dreams of a corpse, it means that his reputation will be ruined, he will fail in business or go bankrupt. If a young man dreams of a corpse, it suggests unrequited love.

Corridor — If an unknown corridor appears in a dream, it is a sign that the dreamer must make an important decision which is not influenced by external factors.

Crabs — Crabs symbolize good health. A single crab symbolizes betrayal.

Crib — An empty crib speaks of a lack of confidence or health problems. Rocking a baby in a crib indicates marital problems.

Crime — An encounter with a criminal in a dream warns of questionable individuals. If the dreamer himself appears as a criminal, it is a sign that he is not sufficiently aware of the hardships of others.

Crocodile — This signifies that someone close to the dreamer is behaving in an exceptionally friendly manner; however, beneath this hearty exterior, he is plotting to harm him.

Crying — Crying in a dream generally heralds good tidings and indicates that there will be reasons for rejoicing and celebrating. However, at times, it may be seen as a signal of distress from a friend.

Cucumber — The dreamer will become ill with a serious disease in the near future.

Cup — A cup full of liquid is a sign of good luck. An empty cup signifies shortage. A dark-colored cup indicates problems at work or in business. A light-colored cup symbolizes a bright future. A cup out of which liquid has spilled predicts fighting and tension in the family.

Currants (red) — The dreamer is avoiding someone whom he is unable to confront. Picking currents is an indication of the dreamer's optimistic personality: the ability always to look on the bright side.

Cursing — If the dreamer curses, it suggests that his goals and objectives will be attained after a particularly big effort. If the dreamer is being cursed by someone else, it means that there are enemies conspiring against him.

Curtain — Closing a curtain in a dream means that people who are close to the dreamer are plotting against him and deceiving him.

Cutting — This indicates an unhealthy connection with someone close to the dreamer. Cutting oneself indicates family problems.

Cyclamen — For men, a dream about this flower symbolizes impotence. For women, it signifies the inability to forge healthy relationships with men.

D

Daffodil — A daffodil indicates that the dreamer suffers from problems relating to his sexual identity.

Dagger — This signifies that the dreamer does not trust those around him.

Daisy — A daisy predicts good times accompanied by happiness and inner confidence.

Dancing — This is a sign of vitality, love of the good life, sexiness and health.

Danger — This signifies success: the greater the danger in the dream, the greater the success in reality.

Darkness — The appearance of darkness, or walking in the dark, indicates that the dreamer is distressed, confused and restless.

Dark-Skinned Person — Dreaming about a dark-skinned person suggests that the dreamer does not have tension and excitement in his life. It may also indicate that he has difficulties resulting from sexual tension.

Dates (fruit) — These predict the marriage of the dreamer or of one of his close friends in the near future.

Deafness — A symbol: What we do not know cannot hurt us!

Death — Contrary to what one might expect, dreaming about death heralds a long and good life. Dreaming about the death of person who is actually ill means that he will recover soon.

Deer — This symbolizes the father figure or the desire to resemble someone who is close to you and who constitutes an authority figure.

Depression — Dreaming about depression indicates the opposite: the dreamer will have a golden opportunity to extricate himself from his present situation and improve his life unrecognizably.

Desert — If the dreamer is walking in the desert, it predicts a journey. If a storm breaks out during the dream, it means that the journey will not be satisfactory. If the dreamer is in the desert and is suffering from hunger and thirst, it means he needs to invigorate his life.

Devil — This actually foretells an easier and better future.

Diamond — This signifies domestic quarrels or confusion and disorder in the dreamer's family life.

Diary — This symbolizes excessive acquisitiveness or a pathological jealousy of someone close to the dreamer.

Dice — Dice symbolize gambling. If the dreamer's financial situation is actually good, it means that he will profit substantially from gambling, and vice versa.

Digestion — Dreaming about the digestive system, one of its components or the sensations connected to it, indicates health problems. (See also **Digestive System**).

Digestive System — Any dream concerning the digestive system (including vomiting and diarrhea) is a sign of health or nutritional problems.

Dirt — Dreaming about dirt, particularly if it appears on clothing, means that certain health problems must be attended to. Dreaming about falling into dirt or garbage predicts that the dreamer will move house in the near future. (See also **Stains**.)

Disabled Person/Cripple — Any dream about a disabled person (the nature or level of disability is irrelevant) attests to the fact that the dreamer's conscience is urging him to help others less fortunate than himself.

Disaster — This is an indication of enemies plotting against the dreamer, particularly in the workplace, and advises him to seek protection from them.

Distress — If the dreamer is in distress, it is a sign that his financial situation will improve substantially.

Divorce — Some claim that dreaming about divorce indicates sexual problems. If the dreamer is married, it means that he is happily married. If a single person who has a partner dreams about divorce, it means that he feels insecure about the relationship.

Doctor — Seeing a doctor in a clinic indicates an urgent need for help. If the dreamer meets the doctor at a social gathering, it is a sign of good health.

Dog — This signifies that the dreamer has a desperate need for security in his relationships with others, and indicates his willingness to enjoy the protection provided by another person.

Dolphin — The dreamer is seeking solutions to problems in the realm of magic and mysticism. It also suggests that the dreamer is removed from reality.

Dominoes — Winning a game of dominoes indicates that the dreamer enjoys being appreciated by others and receiving compliments. Losing a game of dominoes means that the dreamer's problems also trouble others.

Donkey — The braying of a donkey means that the dreamer is in a process of overcoming a painful family relationship. Leading a donkey by a rope attests to the strength of the dreamer's will power. If the dreamer is a child, it means he needs friends.

Door — A closed door warns of wastefulness and

extravagance. An open door, through which people can enter and leave, suggests that the dreamer will soon experience economic difficulties due to poor business management. A revolving door indicates surprises and new experiences.

Doorman (in a hotel or luxury building) — This signifies the dreamer's fierce longing to go on trips to other countries; alternatively, it shows the desire to make far-reaching changes in one's life.

Dough — This is a symbol of wealth, money and property.

Dove — This attests to a happy family life and great economic success. A flock of doves portends a journey or long trip.

Dragon — A dragon means that in times of distress, the dreamer turns to a higher power for help, and does not himself make any effort on his own part to improve his situation. If the dreamer is young, a dragon is a sign of an upcoming wedding.

Drinking — Drinking alcoholic beverages indicates financial loss. If the dreamer sees himself drunk, he can expect great success. Drinking water, however, predicts being let down by someone close.

Driving — If the dreamer is the driver, it means that he feels the need to act independently in life. If another person is driving, it is a sign that the dreamer trusts him. A dream about speeding intimates that the dreamer suffers from emotional problems.

Drowning — If the dreamer sees himself drowning, it is a sign that cooperation with a professional colleague will be profitable. If the dreamer sees other people drowning, it foretells bad things in the future.

Duck — This symbolizes happiness and good luck.

Dwarf — This is an indication of good tidings. A sick or wounded dwarf suggests that the dreamer has hidden enemies.

Dying — If the dreamer sees himself dying in a dream, it indicates a bad conscience or guilt feelings. If another person is dying, it means that the dreamer is trying to shake off feelings of responsibility for that person.

E

Eagle — An eagle in a dream is not to be taken lightly. It is quite significant and indicates an extraordinary desire on the part of the dreamer to fulfill his potential.

Earth — Earth symbolizes abundance and good things awaiting the dreamer. Arid land indicates disrespect of others and the need for soul-searching.

Eating — This heralds confidence and economic stability. Eating together with another person signifies enduring friendship.

Eavesdropping — If others are eavesdropping on the dreamer, it warns of trouble. If the dreamer is eavesdropping on others, he can expect happy surprises!

Edifice — The meaning of the dream lies in the height of the edifice. Average height indicates changes in the near future. A higher-than-average edifice portends brilliant success in the near future.

Egg — The appearance of an egg or the eating of an egg indicates that the dreamer will soon increase his wealth and become more established in life. A broken or rotten egg portends failure or loss.

Eggs — Dreaming about a number of eggs means improvement in the dreamer's financial situation. Two eggs in a nest attests to the support of a loving family. Three eggs in a nest indicate an addition to the family!

Egg Yolk — Good times are on the way. If a gambler dreams of the yolk of an egg, it means that he will have success at gambling.

Elbow — This indicates that the dreamer is involved in activities that do not do justice to his abilities.

Elephant — This predicts that the dreamer will meet people who will become his friends.

Elevator — If the elevator is ascending, it means that the dreamer is yearning for positive changes in his life. A descending elevator indicates the absence of financial success and a lack of initiative.

Emptiness — An empty container or a feeling of emptiness warns of a bitter disappointment that the dreamer will have to cope with and that will weaken him severely, both physically and mentally.

Engagement — This foretells temporary disagreements with one's partner that will be resolved.

Envelope — A sealed envelope indicates hardship, complexes, frustration and difficulties. An open envelope signifies that the dreamer will overcome obstacles that are not too formidable.

Envy/Jealousy — If the dreamer is envious of another person, it predicts possible disappointment. If another person is envious of the dreamer, it heralds success and good luck.

Eulogy — This is a sign of good news (usually marriage) brought by a close friend.

Eve and the Apple — Dreaming about the story of Eve in the Garden of Eden usually symbolizes the dreamer's ability to withstand temptation.

Evening — Dreaming of a pleasant evening predicts that the dreamer will soon enjoy a period of tranquillity and calm.

Explosion — This means that one of the dreamer's friends is in danger.

Eye Doctor — This warns the dreamer to keep his eyes open and be aware of his situation in order not to miss any opportunities that present themselves.

Eyeglasses/Binoculars — These indicate that the dreamer will experience a great improvement in his life, as things that were previously unclear to him will be clarified and understood.

F

Face — Seeing his face in a mirror indicates to the dreamer that in the near future he will be privy to secrets that will influence his life significantly.

Failure — Contrary to what might be expected, this actually predicts success and overcoming obstacles.

Fair/Bazaar — Dreaming about being at a fair means that the dreamer must maintain a low profile in the near future and not be conspicuous.

Fame — A dream about fame, whether that of the dreamer or of somebody close to him, warns of events that will be a source of nervousness and restlessness.

Fan — An elaborate fan signifies that the dreamer is arrogant and egocentric. A new fan predicts good news. An old fan indicates that there is reason to be concerned about serious incidents or unpleasant news.

Farm/Ranch — A walk around a farm means success in business. If the dreamer is in love, a happy relationship can be expected.

Farmer — This suggests a life of prosperity and abundance; success in all areas: economic, social, personal and health.

Father — When the dreamer is addressed by his father, joyful events will soon occur in his life. If the father merely appears in the dream, worries and problems can be expected.

Fatigue — This warns against making incorrect decisions that the dreamer will regret all his life.

Faucet — A faucet with water flowing out of it indicates business growth and financial success.

Fence — Breaking down a fence in a dream is a sign that problems will be resolved in the near future. If a young woman dreams of a fence, it indicates that she is longing to be married and have children. A green fence signifies true love.

Fern — This indicates an unusually strong sexual appetite.

Fever — A high fever warns against wrongful actions and deeds which bring negative results.

Fig — A fig is a prediction of good news.

Finger — A hurt finger indicates a wounded self-image. The hurt finger of another person indicates incitement, vicious gossip or slander, all directed against the dreamer.

Fire — This warns of problems that might arise in the vicinity of the dreamer.

Fireplace —This is indicative of an upcoming period of prosperity, growth and economic stability for the dreamer.

Fish — A single fish heralds success or means that the dreamer has a particularly successful and brilliant child. A school of fish means that the dreamer's friends care about him and are doing things for his benefit. Fishing in a dream signifies treachery on the part of a friend or friends. Eating fish predicts success following hard work.

Fish Eggs — A sign of serenity and comfort for the dreamer.

Flag — This means that the dreamer has a pleasant and tranquil character. Waving a flag in a contest means that the dreamer should take a break from the rat race and rest. A torn flag indicates disgrace.

Flash Flood — This is an indication of danger on the horizon. Overcoming a flash flood or strong stream of water indicates overcoming obstacles and achieving success as a result of hard work.

Fleas — Fleas mean that the dreamer's life is chaotic and extremely disorganized.

Floating — Dreaming about floating in the air is very common. It usually indicates that the dreamer should focus his efforts on one objective.

Flood/Heavy Rain — This symbolizes hardship and the inability to reach an understanding with one's surroundings.

Flowers — Picking flowers in a dream signifies that the dreamer may count on his friends not to let him down.

Throwing flowers in a dream is a prediction of a quarrel with someone close to him in the future. If the dream is about arranging flowers, a pleasant surprise can be expected.

Flute — If the dreamer himself is playing the flute, it is an indication of hidden musical talent. Listening to the flute being played by somebody else means that the dreamer can rely on his friends.

Fly (insect) — This indicates everyday worries and concerns.

Flying — If the dreamer sees himself flying in the sky, it indicates that he does not have both feet firmly planted on the ground. He is not aware of his serious financial situation and ought to save more money and rethink his economic strategies.

Fog — If the dreamer is in fog, it is a sign that his plans will be fulfilled. If fog is seen from afar, it indicates disagreement between the dreamer and those close to him.

Folder/Binder — This means that the dreamer needs to consult with friends or receive assistance from them.

Food — If the dreamer sees himself eating and enjoying himself, it heralds good and happy times to come: His aspirations will be realized!

Foot — When a person's foot appears in a dream, it means that the dreamer suffers from physical ailments which stem from his mind.

Forest — Entering a dense forest suggests problems in the near future, particularly in the financial realm.

Fortress — If the dreamer is inside a fortress, it means that he possesses a burning desire to become rich. If a fortress is seen in the distance, it suggests frustration and a feeling of having missed out. If the dreamer lives in the fortress, it means that the dreamer will acquire much wealth.

Fox — This indicates that the dreamer is esteemed by those around him and enjoys a good reputation. If the dreamer chases a fox, it means that he is divorced from reality.

Friend — If a friend appears in a dream, it means that he is in trouble or in danger.

Frogs — These symbolize a good, happy and carefree life.

Fruit — This is usually a prediction of good and pleasant things for the dreamer in the future.

Fruit (dried) — A warning: The dreamer was not cautious when taking a certain stand, or he made a hasty decision.

Fuel/Gasoline — A warning: The dreamer must distance himself from any situation which might lead to a confrontation with those close to him.

Fur — Dry fur predicts wealth, good luck and happiness. Wet fur heralds success only after an about-face in one's life.

G

Gaiety — A dream of especially great merriment, laughter and joy actually warns of hard times ahead.

Gaining Weight — This predicts bad times for the dreamer in the near future.

Galloping — Galloping on a horse confirms that the dreamer is on a direct path to success.

Gambling — Actively gambling at a table in a dream symbolizes a future loss in business.

Game — If the dreamer is participating in a competitive game, it means that he will soon receive good, happy news. If the dreamer is just watching a game, it means that in reality, he is very jealous of one of his friends.

Gang — This reflects the dreamer's profound need for belonging and intimacy. A violent meeting with members of a gang suggests a fear of intimacy and close relationships.

Garden — Good tidings: a successful marriage, economic prosperity and material abundance. A garden with blooming flowers symbolizes an expanding business and inner peace. A vegetable garden indicates the need to take precautionary measures.

Garlic — Dreaming of garlic is interpreted according to the dreamer's taste: If he likes garlic, it is a positive dream predicting success. If he is revolted by garlic, it portends bad times.

Gate — A closed gate indicates social problems. A broken gate means problems on the ladder of promotion at work. If the dreamer sees himself swinging on the gate, it means that he prefers resting to working.

Gazelle — This signifies that the dreamer is a loner.

Germ — This is an indication of the dreamer's hypochondria and constant fear of illness.

Getting Lost — This attests to frustration, embarrassment, confusion and a general dissatisfaction with life, especially regarding a romantic relationship in which the dreamer is involved.

Ghost — The appearance of a ghost and a conversation with it indicate difficulties coping with someone's death and the desire to make contact with the world of the dead.

Giant — This is a sign of the dreamer's ability to cope with and overcome problems, despite the hardships involved. It may also be an indication of an emotional problem that manifests itself mainly in feelings of inferiority.

Gift — If the dreamer receives a gift from somebody, it means that the latter is plotting against him, attempting to deceive and undermine him.

Giraffe — This signifies serious sexual problems, particularly if the dreamer is a single man.

Glory — This is a sign that the dreamer has reached the peak of his achievements and from here on it is downhill all the way.

Gloves — Losing gloves means a loss of control in business or a financial loss due to incorrect decision-making.

Glue — This signifies confidence and a senior position in the workplace. If the dream is about fixing objects with glue, it is a warning about financial problems.

Goat — This symbolizes virility. It sometimes foretells a substantial reward for hard work.

God — If one dreams about God as an abstraction, as a concrete object (such as a religious sculpture) or as a deity image, or if one dreams of any kind of ritual, this reflects the dreamer's connection to religion. A dream of God heralds serenity, stability and security.

Gold — Finding gold in a dream means that the dreamer will accomplish great things and attain the goals which he has set for himself. Losing gold means that the dreamer underestimates important issues. Touching gold means that the dreamer will take up a new hobby or occupation.

Goose — A warning: The dreamer's expectations will not be fulfilled. If he dreams about killing a goose, great success can be expected.

Grapefruit — This is an indication of health problems and a lack of energy and vitality.

Grapes — These symbolize hedonism and the pursuit of pleasure.

Grass — This indicates that whatever the dreamer desires is within his reach. There is no need for him to wander far off, as it is within his grasp. Green lawns indicate that wishes and expectations will be fulfilled.

Grasshopper — A threat is hanging over the dreamer's head.

Grave — Dreaming about a grave symbolizes everything the dreamer is lacking: health for a sick person, money for someone of limited means, marriage for single people, etc.

Grove — If one dreams about a grove, particularly a green grove, it means that life will change for the better. A dying grove (as a result of fire or disease) means that the dreamer should make provision for his old age.

Guidance/Instruction — This means that in the near future there is likely to be an encounter with a person who has a positive influence over the dreamer.

Gun/Pistol — Dreaming of a shot from a pistol suggests

a lack of progress in business, as well as stagnation. The dreamer must change his ways in order to alter the trend.

Gutter (of a roof) — The gutter in all its forms means that the dreamer can expect a long and worry-free life. Climbing up a gutter-pipe indicates that the dreamer wants to run away from solving his problems.

Gypsy — A warning: The dreamer must watch out for a swindler who will make him suffer in the future. If the dreamer himself appears as a gypsy, it is a sign that in the future he will wander to another land to seek happiness.

H

Hair — Thick, healthy hair means that the dreamer will soon be involved in successful projects. A dream about unusually colored hair indicates anxiety, hesitation and suspicion.

Hairdresser — Dreaming about a hairdresser reflects the dreamer's dejection and depression.

Hammer — The dreamer should consider his steps carefully and not waste money.

Hand — A dirty hand means that the dreamer is facing a difficult period in his life. A **bound hand** indicates that his sadness will turn into happiness and joy.

Handcuffs — These symbolize an impossible relationship or problems related to the judicial system. A dream of being released from handcuffs means that the dreamer is not an ordinary person.

Handicap — If the dreamer dreams that he is handicapped, he can expect an improvement in his status and in other areas of life. Overcoming a handicap means that the dreamer will overcome obstacles along his path; the opposite is true as well.

Handkerchief — Searching for a handkerchief in a dream is a sign of an imminent separation. If a handkerchief is found easily, it means that the dreamer will soon receive a gift.

Hanging — If the dreamer sees himself being hanged, it indicates a promising career. If another person is being hanged, it means that one of the dreamer's acquaintances will become famous.

Happiness — Contrary to what it seems, dreaming of happiness forecasts times of hardship and danger, particularly at the workplace.

Harp — Hearing the sound of a harp attests to the dreamer's melancholy nature. A broken harp means that he has health problems. If he himself is playing the harp, it is a warning that he is a victim of some sort of deception connected to his love life.

Harvest — One of the best images that can appear in a dream. It predicts economic, domestic and social success.

Hat — If the dreamer wears a hat, it signifies imminent disappointment. If he loses a hat, it means he will soon receive a gift. Finding a hat in a dream is a sign that the dreamer will soon lose a small item. The inability to remove one's hat is a warning of disease.

Head — If the dreamer sees himself wounded in the head, it is a sign that he has hidden enemies.

Headache — This indicates that one of the dreamer's friends needs his help.

Headlights — If the dreamer is blinded by the headlights of a car, it means that he should take steps quickly in order to prevent possible complications.

Heart — Any type of dream about a heart heralds good tidings in all areas of life.

Heaviness — A feeling of heaviness means that the dreamer is grappling with heavy and fateful issues.

Heel — A broken heel means that the dreamer will have to confront problems and hardship in the near future.

Hell — This indicates that the dreamer is greedy and materialistic, and what preoccupies him most is money. A dream about hell does not bode well. Financial losses can be expected, much to the joy of the dreamer's enemies.

Hen/Rooster — A hen with chicks indicates the need to plan ahead with precision before acting. Hearing a rooster in a dream indicates exaggerated self-confidence.

Heron — This suggests a change occurring in the dreamer's life. Some interpret the heron as a symbol of stagnation, lack of development and being stuck in a rut.

Hiding-Place — If the dreamer hides in a hiding-place, it is a sign that he will soon receive bad news.

Hippopotamus — This warns of being overweight or refers to feelings of inferiority.

Honey — This symbolizes happiness and joy. The dreamer will attain his objectives and enjoy the fruits of his labor and efforts.

Honor — This is a sign that the dreamer must take precautions in money matters and adopt more economical patterns of behavior.

Horn (animal) — Dreaming about an animal's horn signifies sexual problems. The interpretation of the dream depends on the context in which the horn appears.

Horse — Dreaming about a horse symbolizes passion or lust; riding a white horse - business and social success; riding a black horse - failure; a runaway horse - financial losses; falling off a horse - a hasty, rushed marriage; riding a wild horse - strong sexual passion.

Horse-Race — If the dreamer is a woman, it indicates imminent marital problems. If the dreamer is a man, it warns of danger from an unexpected source. The dreamer must take care and beware. (See also **Horse**.)

Horseshoe — This means that the dreamer will embark on a sea voyage in the near future.

Hospital — If a healthy person dreams about a hospital, it means that he fears disease and death. Dreaming about being treated in a hospital by a medical staff indicates fear of the future.

Hotel —This means that the dreamer is in need of changes in his life. It also warns against making hasty decisions.

Hot Pepper — This reflects feelings of pride resulting from the success of someone close to the dreamer.

Hugging — Hugging, particularly a family member or a person close to the dreamer, reflects his need to give of himself to others.

Hunchback — This indicates imminent success.

I

Ice-Skating — This has two meanings in a dream: It warns of flattery, or of an unstable relationship with the person whom the dreamer loves most.

Insect (crawling) — Despite unpleasant connotations, a significant, positive change can be expected in the dreamer's life.

Insect — This symbolizes difficulties and disappointments in the business or family life of the dreamer.

Insult — This indicates that the dreamer yearns for change in his life (in his job or place of residence).

Intersection — This signifies exactly that: The dreamer has come to a crossroad in his life and must make decisions that will affect his destiny.

Interview — An interview suggests that there will soon be a promotion and good news from a close acquaintance.

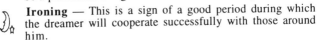 **Ironing** — This is a sign of a good period during which the dreamer will cooperate successfully with those around him.

Ivy — This indicates that the dreamer is sensitive and dedicated to the traditions he grew up with and to the people close to him.

J

Jasmine — This indicates that the dreamer is not exploiting even a fraction of his talents and abilities.

Jewelry — This is a sign that that the dreamer is lucky. Broken jewelry portends disappointment. Receiving jewelry as a gift signifies a happy marriage. Losing jewelry in a dream suggests troubles caused by gambling.

Journey — This means that the dreamer may expect changes in his life.

Judge — This clearly indicates that the dreamer must not be quick to judge other people or determine their guilt or innocence.

Jug — A jug is a symbol of good luck. If the jug is full, this is extremely good luck.

Jumping — Jumping in a dream is not a good sign: it means the dreamer can expect hardships, disappointment or frustration.

K

Kangaroo — This means the dreamer is not satisfied with one partner.

Kennel/Doghouse — This indicates emotional stress and a lack of serenity. It warns of health problems and physical weakness.

Kettle — If the kettle has boiled, it warns against loss of assets. If the water has not yet boiled, it predicts success and good luck.

Key — Any situation involving a key (except the loss of a key) is good news: success in one's personal, social, financial and family life. The loss of a key is a warning of things to come.

King — If a king appears or speaks to the dreamer, it means good things or a change for the better in the dreamer's life.

Kiss — If the dreamer is kissing a stranger, it is a sign that he is not completely aware of what is going on around him, and this could do him great harm.

Kitchen — This appears mainly in women's dreams. It attests to satisfaction with family life and loyal friends.

Kite — Flying a kite in a dream indicates that the dreamer enjoys sharing his feelings with others and that he will attain all of his objectives in life.

Knee — An uninjured knee signifies success and happiness. An injured knee indicates a need to deal with difficulties that will put the dreamer's patience to the test.

Knife — Dreaming about a knife is usually a warning. Any type of knife can only mean bad times: domestic quarrels, lack of understanding, violent outbursts and fears.

Knight — Dreaming about a knight indicates that the dreamer is bothered by issues of status and hierarchy, as well as the relationship between the ruler and the ruled.

Knitting — A dream about knitting anything is a sign of a good life. If the knitting needle or the ball of wool falls down, it warns of enemies.

Knot — Any knot in a dream is a sign of economic problems and financial losses.

L

Label — If a label or sticker indicating a name or an item appears, it heralds a future full of surprises.

Ladder — If the dreamer climbs a ladder without mishap, it is a sign that his ambitions are about to be realized. Fear of ascending a ladder, or an accident (such as falling off the ladder) is a dire prediction. A ladder leaning against a wall means that one of the dreamer's relatives is disloyal to him.

Ladybug — If this red insect with the black dots appears, it is a sign that the dreamer will soon chance upon a golden opportunity which will allow him to fulfill his greatest dreams.

Lake — The dreamer is soon to enjoy the fruits of his past labors. Positive developments in his life can be expected.

Lamp/Flashlight — A bright lamp means that the dreamer is a honest person and seeks justice. A dim lamp indicates a feeling of embarrassment and confusion.

Landing (from flight) — This predicts hardships for the dreamer in the near future. However, he will overcome them.

Lark — This is a sign of joyous events and a perfect marriage for the dreamer.

Lateness — If the dreamer is late, despite his attempts to arrive on time, it attests to the fact that people value his opinion and are waiting to hear what he has to say.

Laughter — The dreamer's laughter is actually an indication of sad things that he is liable to experience. If others are laughing, it is a sign that the dreamer's life will be happy and full of joy.

Laundry — A warning: Failure and domestic problems will arise soon.

Laurels — This is a rare image symbolizing forthcoming honor, glory and fame in the dreamer's life.

Law — All the elements relating to the law (including courts, police, lawyers, etc.) give the dreamer a warning: Think carefully before making a decision concerning financial issues.

Lawsuit — This means that the dreamer has a conservative nature: He lives a full and serene life, but is not spontaneous and does not break his routine easily.

Lawyer — This means that the dreamer is in need of assistance, advice and guidance.

Leaves — If one dreams about a tree with green leaves, it is a sign that one's love life will improve. Withered leaves mean that the dreamer is frustrated with a bad decision he made.

Lecture — If the dreamer is giving a lecture in front of an audience, it indicates that he will enjoy great professional success.

Leg — If the dreamer's legs are emphasized, it means that he is rational, self-aware, and has a lot of self-confidence.

Legumes — These symbolize economic success and prosperity in business.

Lemon — This signifies despair resulting from a great love for and disappointment in one's partner.

Leopard — A warning: An enemy is attempting to harm the dreamer - and may succeed.

Letter — Writing or receiving a letter in a dream means that unexpected good news is on its way.

Lettuce — This is an indication of problems relating to sexuality and a person's love life in general.

Lice — These signify that the dreamer suffers from feelings of social alienation or inferiority.

Lie — If the dreamer or another person lies in a dream, it is a warning to beware of a shady deal or fraud.

Light — The meaning of the dream changes according to the intensity of the light. A bright, shining light - wealth and happiness; a dull light - disappointment and depression; a green light - the dreamer's jealousy.

Lightning — This dream heralds particularly good tidings, especially concerning agriculture and farming.

Lily — The lily is considered a symbol of holiness amongst Christians and is connected to holy sites and people.

Limping — If the dreamer is limping, it is a sign that he will always have friends around him. If another person is limping, it is a sign that the dreamer is about to be bitterly disappointed.

Line — If the dreamer is standing on line, this indicates that a relationship with an old friend, severed due to an argument, will be soon renewed.

Lion — This is a sign that one of the dreamer's friends will be very successful; in the future, the dreamer will benefit highly from this success and will receive help from the friend.

Lips — Fleshy lips signify happiness and joy for the dreamer. Thin, pale lips are an indication of anguish and pain.

Lizard — This is a warning that a person with bad intentions is conspiring against the dreamer, and he should be careful.

Loan — If someone requests a loan from the dreamer, it means that the latter will soon suffer considerable financial losses. If the dreamer is unsuccessful in his attempt to pay back a loan, it is a good sign, foretelling an improvement in his economic situation.

Loss — Losses, wounds or injuries are interpreted as warning signs. Be alert to and aware of changes in life or to any situation fraught with potential danger.

Love — If an unmarried person dreams of love, it indicates marriage in the near future. If the dreamer is married, it predicts a domestic quarrel. A dream about a couple's relationship in general — one that is based on pure intentions — hints at happiness, joy and success. If the dream relationship is based on exploitation, it symbolizes disappointment in reality.

M

Machines — Machines used for production or other sophisticated machinery indicate complex problems in all areas of life.

Madness — A dream about madness of any kind is actually a sign of particularly good luck, predicting happiness, prosperity and success.

Magic — This predicts changes for the better in the dreamer's life, especially in finance and health.

Man/Woman — Dreaming about a man indicates good things. Dreaming about a woman represents a warning to think carefully before making an important or fateful decision.

Manager/Boss — Any dream about a manager or boss, whether the dreamer himself is the manager or another person is the boss, indicates a promotion at work, as well as improvement in economic and social status.

Mansion — If the dreamer enters a mansion, he can expect good news. If he leaves a mansion in a hurry, it predicts serious problems that await him.

Map — This is a sign that the dreamer can expect some kind of change in his life.

Marching — Marching along an uneven road suggests misunderstandings and a lack of communication with the dreamer's surroundings.

Marriage/Nuptials — Dreaming about marriage, particularly if the groom is elegantly dressed, is a sign of a great disappointment that awaits the dreamer, or of a significant decrease in his status.

Mask — This signifies that the dreamer is two-faced. It also warns him of betrayal by a person close to him who is acting behind his back in an attempt to undermine him.

Meat — If the dreamer cooks, it means good tidings. If he eats meat prepared by someone else, he can expect bad times.

Medicine — Any kind of medicine in a dream signifies that in the near future, the dreamer's life will be temporarily upset by worries and hardships.

Medium (clairvoyant) — Dreams about an individual who acts as an intermediary between the world of the living and the world of the dead predict that the dreamer will undergo a serious crisis in the near future.

Melon — This means that the dreamer can expect changes for the better in his life.

Mermaid — Dreaming about something that does not exist in reality signifies the search for impossible love.

Milk — Purchasing milk portends good times; selling milk - success and good luck; boiling milk - success following great effort; sour and spoiled milk - domestic problems.

Millstone — This represents hard work for which there is not sufficient remuneration.

Mint (plant) — Dreaming about mint means good news: the dreamer will soon receive a substantial inheritance from an unexpected source.

Mole — This is a warning of danger hovering over the dreamer's head.

Money — Finding money is a sign of a unique opportunity that was missed. Winning money means that the dreamer should consider his actions carefully. Stealing money indicates a fear of losing authority.

Monk/Nun — This indicates that the dreamer's problems or troubles will soon be resolved and that the dreamer will enjoy a period of tranquillity and serenity.

Monkey — This means that the dreamer has a dishonest relationship with a close acquaintance.

Monster — A monster appearing in different forms in a dream signifies that the dreamer suffers from extreme fear to the point of paralysis.

Moon — This symbolizes outstanding success in love.

Mosquito — This is a sign that enemies are plotting evil against the dreamer.

Moth — A relationship with someone close with the dreamer will become strained.

Mother — The nature of the relationship between the dreamer and his mother is of the utmost importance. Usually, dreaming about a mother speaks of pregnancy in the near future. However, it may also symbolize strong friendship, honesty, wisdom, generosity and a successful married life.

Mother-in-law — If the dreamer argues with his mother-in-law, it means that he wants peace at home.

Motor — This symbolizes the desire to be a leader and to be at the center of things.

Mountain — If the ascent is very difficult, it portends

encounters with obstacles that the dreamer will struggle to overcome. An easy, fast ascent means that the dreamer possesses the ability to cope with crises successfully. If he meets other people during the climb, it signifies that the dreamer will have to seek help from others on his path to success.

Mourning — This symbolizes loss, sorrow and pain.

Mouse — This warns of potential harm to the dreamer as a result of unnecessary interference by others in his life.

Mouth — A big mouth means great future wealth. A small mouth means financial problems.

Mud — Dreaming about mud symbolizes dissatisfaction. Extricating oneself from mud or quicksand represents the ability to get out of difficult and complex situations.

Mushrooms — These signify that the dreamer will soon forge significant social bonds.

Music — Harmonious and pleasant music symbolizes success and a good life. Discordant and cacophonous sounds signal disruptions during a journey or long trip.

Mustard — A warning: Beware of taking bad advice.

Mute/Dumb — This indicates that the dreamer must keep a secret, or else he will suffer harm.

N

Nails (finger) — Long nails mean happiness with one's spouse and success in business. Short nails warn of financial losses.

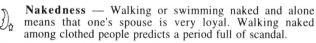

Nakedness — Walking or swimming naked and alone means that one's spouse is very loyal. Walking naked among clothed people predicts a period full of scandal.

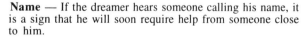

Name — If the dreamer hears someone calling his name, it is a sign that he will soon require help from someone close to him.

Narrow Passage — A feeling of suffocation and a lack of air while dreaming of being in a narrow passage signifies the dreamer's very strong sexual passion or feelings of pressure and anxiety.

Neck — A dream about receiving a compliment about one's neck signifies that one has a full love life.

Necklace — This symbolizes the dreamer's desire to be at the center of things. Losing a necklace indicates hard times in the near future.

Needle — Finding a needle in a dream predicts a strong friendship with a new acquaintance. Threading a needle symbolizes the dreamer's responsible nature. A broken needle is a sign of acceptance and reconciliation. Sewing means that the dreamer suffers from loneliness.

Nervousness — Good news is on the way!

News — Strangely, good news in a dream warns of problems and worries. Bad news, however, heralds good luck and success in the near future.

Newspaper — This means that the dreamer's reputation is being compromised.

Night — Darkness and night symbolize a lack of mental clarity, as well as confusion and a lack of clarity in the dreamer's life.

Nightingale — The nightingale sparks an immediate association with melody and pleasant sounds. It means that romance will dominate the dreamer's life for a short while.

Noise — If there is a lot of noise around the dreamer, it means that he will play the role of arbiter and peacemaker in a quarrel between two people close to him.

Nomad — If the dreamer or another person appears as a nomad or a wanderer, he has a burning desire for change in his life.

Nose — If the dreamer sees himself with a large nose in a dream, it indicates great wealth and economic prosperity. A small nose means that one of the dreamer's immediate family members or relatives will disgrace the family.

Note — If the dreamer receives a note, it means that although he requires his friends' help, they will not offer it.

Notebook — The dreamer has problems breaking away from his past.

Nurse — If a nurse appears in a dream, it suggests good things to come - mainly success at work or an improvement in one's economic situation.

O

Oak — The oak tree is a symbol of health and a good quality of life.

Oats — A horse eating oats indicates that the dreamer has unfinished tasks at hand.

Ocean — This signifies a desire for a new beginning, or for withdrawal and inner contemplation. A calm sea and a clear horizon represent a rosy future; a stormy sea predicts imminent danger.

Office — If the dreamer works in an office, financial problems are predicted. Managing an office symbolizes ambitiousness and the ability to overcome obstacles.

Officer — This indicates that the dreamer needs an authoritative figure in his life to map a path for him.

Oil — A man's dream about oil represents a warning against difficult times, fraught with disappointments and frustration. If a woman dreams about oil, she will be respected and have a happy marriage.

Olive — The olive symbolizes happiness and wealth for the dreamer. A dream about harvesting olives or about black olives predicts a birth in the family.

Onion — This is an indication of difficulties, economic concerns, fear of losses. Peeling an onion symbolizes renewed efforts to try and achieve a coveted objective.

Opera — A dream of an opera that is unpleasant to the dreamer's ears is a sign of crisis and failure, conflict and inner turmoil. If the dreamer participates in an opera, it symbolizes a desire to reveal a hidden talent that has not yet come to the fore.

Opponent/Rival — A dream about an opponent is a sign that the dreamer's wishes will soon come true.

Orange — Eating or seeing an orange in a dream suggests a significant improvement in one's lifestyle.

Orchard — If the orchard is surrounded by a fence, it means that the dreamer yearns for something unattainable.

Orchestra — Listening to an orchestra playing music indicates that the dreamer will be very famous. A dream about playing in an orchestra predicts a significant promotion at work.

Orchid — This attests to the dreamer's strong sexual desires.

Orphanhood — If the dreamer or another person is orphaned, it means that a new and positive personality will enter the dreamer's life, constituting a highly dominant force.

Ostrich — This is a sign that the dreamer or a family member has health problems.

Oven — The dreamer is in need of warm and loving human contact.

Owl — This symbolizes sad things: melancholy, pain, loss, etc.

P

Package — Receiving a package means that there are positive changes in store for the dreamer or for those close to him.

Packing — This indicates a yearning for change. If the dreamer does not finish packing, it is a sign of frustration.

Pain — This shows that the dreamer is surrounded by a supportive and loving environment. The stronger the pain, the more significant the dreamer is to those around him.

Painting — This indicates that something the dreamer has long been wishing for will come true.

Palace — If the dreamer finds himself in a palace or great hall, it is a sign of unexpected problems. If he did not see the entrance to this place, it means that good news regarding romance is coming his way.

Palms (of the hands) — If the hands are far from the body, it shows that the dreamer and those around him do not understand each other. Hairy palms - the dreamer has a wild imagination; dirty palms - jealousy; folded hands - emotional stress; bound hands - the dreamer is very restrained.

Paper (sheets) — Sheets of paper signify restlessness and a lack of clarity. The cleaner and lighter the sheets, the greater the chance of extricating oneself from the problematic situation and turning over a new leaf.

Paradise — This indicates a change for the better in life. The transition will manifest itself in a move from preoccupation with the material world to preoccupation with the spiritual world.

Parents — Parent-child relationships indicate various family problems (not necessarily with parents).

Parrot — A parrot which is tied up suggests that the dreamer enjoys gossiping or is a victim of gossip.

Peach — Opportunities to enjoy pleasurable experiences can be expected in the future.

Peacock — This warns against conceit and excessive pride.

Peanuts — These signify that the dreamer is sociable and will be blessed with many friends.

Pear — This indicates that others are gossiping and talking about the dreamer, his friends or relatives behind his back.

Peas — These herald a good period, bringing prosperity and economic growth.

Peddler — This predicts financial success occurring in an unusual manner.

Pen — If the dreamer is writing with a pen, he will hear from a person with whom he has been out of touch for a long time.

Penguin — This signifies that the dreamer has an adventurous character and aspires to go on journeys.

Penis — Dreaming about a penis has a sexual interpretation which depends on the character of the dreamer.

Perfume — A dream about perfume is a sign of good news, particularly concerning love relationships.

Pestering/Bothering — Any kind of pestering means that nonsense, useless chatter and small talk are liable to cause harm.

Pheasant — This is a symbol of wealth, well-being and economic prosperity.

Photography — Any sort of photography indicates a long journey. If a woman dreams about a camera, it means that she will soon have a heart-warming meeting with a man.

Picture — This shows a strong desire to succeed and avoid failure.

Pig — In Western culture, a pig symbolizes a difficult personality, one that does not get on well with others. In the Far East, it is a sign of economic abundance.

Pillow — This is a warning against an inappropriate action by the dreamer that may cause concern, embarrassment and a lack of confidence.

Pills — If the dreamer sees pills in a package or a bottle, it means that he will soon embark on a journey or a trip.

Pineapple —This is an indication of days of happiness and joy, especially in the company of close friends.

Pine Cone — A closed pine cone symbolizes a tight-knit family; an open pine cone indicates a family that has separated and drifted apart.

Pleasure Boat — This indicates that the dreamer longs to go on a vacation and let his hair down.

Plum — This is a clear sign that the dreamer has enemies of whom he is not aware.

Pocket — A pocket symbolizes the womb. The dream is interpreted according to the context in which the pocket appeared. It may indicate the dreamer's desire to return to the womb, or, alternatively, his desire to storm back into life.

Police — A dream involving the police on any level means that the dreamer will soon receive assistance which will extricate him from the crisis he is now going through. A dream about confrontation with a policeman or about arrest shows that the dreamer suffers from confusion and guilt.

Pomegranate — A pomegranate or pomegranate tree suggests that the dreamer fears sexual infidelity on the part of his partner.

Porch — If the dreamer stands on a porch, it means that day-to-day worries are bothering him.

Port/Harbor - This symbolizes worries, conflicts with others, dissatisfaction and a lack of serenity.

Postman — This is a sign that the dreamer is worried about financial, business-related or social difficulties.

Post Office — Dreaming of a post office indicates that the dreamer has a guilty conscience concerning an outstanding debt or commitment.

Potato — This symbolizes calm, stability and satisfaction with one's life.

Potsherds — These portend a period of happiness and joy, as well as of economic prosperity.

Prayer — If the dreamer is praying, it is a sign that a good period, filled with happiness and joy, is approaching. If prayer takes place without the dreamer, it is a sign that the dreamer's deeds are harmful to others.

Pregnancy — This is an indication of dissatisfaction with the dreamer's present situation and the longing to turn over a new leaf.

Prince/Princess — This indicates that the dreamer possesses the hidden ability to fulfill his urgent need to improve his social status.

Prison — Dreaming about imprisonment warns about a change for the worse in physical health. A dream about an unsuccessful attempt to escape from prison is an indication of an obstacle in one's life that must be overcome. A dream about a successful escape from prison suggests success and the fulfillment of hopes.

Prize — Winning a prize signifies the opposite: Heavy financial losses can be expected.

Procession/Parade — A festive procession or parade indicate changes that will usher in a period of stormy events.

Profit — If the dreamer receives a large sum of money, this is a sign of deception, denial and being led astray by one of his close friends.

Punch — If the dreamer has punched someone, he should expect to lose a court case. If the dreamer has been punched, he should expect to win.

Q

Quarrel — If the dreamer is involved in a quarrel, it means that someone is fiercely jealous of him. Alternatively, he will be lucky.

Queen — This indicates that the dreamer will soon receive help or assistance from those close to him.

Quicksand — If the dreamer is trapped in quicksand, it is a sign that his social and economic status is improving. If he sees another person trapped in quicksand, it is a sign that others will stand in the way of his attempts to achieve his objectives.

Quitting (a job)/Resignation — Dreaming about quitting a job, especially if the dreamer has a senior position, indicates that his plans will be realized in the near future.

R

Rabbit — If the rabbit is white, it means that the dreamer is sexually unfulfilled and is dissatisfied with his sex life.

Rain — This does not bode well. Gentle, light rain indicates that the dreamer will have to face disappointment and frustration; heavy, pounding rain means that the dreamer will have to cope with situations that will cause him despondency and depression.

Rainbow — This is always a good sign: Happiness, joy, serenity and pleasure will come the dreamer's way.

Raisins — These symbolize wastefulness and extravagance that need to be curbed.

Rake (the tool) — This is an indication of great effort and hard work that must be expected on the road to glory.

Rape — If a woman dreams of rape, it indicates a warped relationship with her partner.

Raspberry — This symbolizes a strong desire for passionate sexual relations.

Rat — This is a sign that a person very close to the dreamer is conspiring against him. If a pack of rats appears, it means that the dreamer's health is very poor.

Raven — This signifies mystical beliefs or black magic.

Recipe — Dreaming about a recipe book indicates that the dreamer is blessed with good physical and mental health.

Recitation — Learning a text by heart is a sign of problems that the dreamer must face and that he will overcome. This dream is a sign of the extraordinary success the dreamer will enjoy on any path that he might choose.

Reconciliation — If the dreamer effects a reconciliation with a person with whom he has fought and severed relations, it suggests good tidings.

Religion — Dreaming of a religious event signifies a positive and successful future: the dreamer will enjoy good times.

Religious Functionary — The appearance of a religious functionary indicates hard times filled with problems, disappointments, anxiety and frustration.

Reptiles — Any kind of reptile is usually a sign of conflicts or obstacles awaiting the dreamer.

Rescue — If the dreamer is rescued in his dream, it indicates that he was misled or mistaken, and warns against making any momentous decisions.

Restaurant — This usually symbolizes love and romance, but may also indicate that the dreamer lacks a warm family relationship. In addition, it may symbolize hedonism and love of the good life.

Revenge — Any sort of revenge in a dream signifies that the dreamer will be guilty of causing a quarrel.

Rhinoceros — This signifies a longing for male potency, as a result of sexual problems.

Ribbon — This is a sign of extravagance. Dreaming about a bride wearing ribbons indicates that the groom's intentions are not honorable.

Rice — Good things can be expected in one's personal or family life: an improvement in one's sex life, finding the perfect partner or domestic harmony.

Riot/Tumult — Displays of violence, rage or wild behavior indicate that the dreamer's conscience is not clear, and that he is advised to reevaluate his actions carefully.

River — If the dreamer is sitting on the bank of a river whose waters are clear, he will soon travel or go on a long trip. A stormy river with muddy water indicates obstacles on his path to success.

Road — Dreaming about a difficult road, winding and full of potholes, is a sign of success in the personal and business realms. A smooth, straight road indicates family quarrels.

Roadblock — This predicts a good period in life. The dreamer can expect a promotion at work and will succeed in attaining his objectives.

Robbery/Theft — This is an indication of fears and anxieties stemming from economic difficulties.

Robin — Dreaming about this bird is usually connected to its red color — the color of sex and love — or suggests an attempt to make amends with a person one loves.

Rock — This symbolizes danger and difficulties. The larger the rock, the greater the danger.

Rocking-Chair — An empty rocking-chair is a sign that sadness and pain are coming the way of the dreamer as a result of separation from a loved one. Someone sitting in a rocking-chair is a sign of material and economic stability, as well as personal happiness.

Roller-Skates — If the dreamer is roller-skating, it is a warning: He may be involved in an accident in the near future, and he should be careful.

Roof — If a roof or the construction of a roof appears in a dream, it shows progress in one's life. Climbing onto a roof is a sign that one's ambitions will be fulfilled. Climbing quickly on to a roof indicates that success will arrive even more quickly. A penthouse apartment indicates success and prosperity.

Room (a closed room) — This symbolizes the dreamer's repressed fears, or his unsatisfactory relationship with his partner.

Rope — If the dreamer sees himself tied up with a rope, it is a sign that he has broken (or is about to break) a promise to a friend or betray a confidence. Climbing a rope suggests difficulties on the road to success. Tying a rope is an indication of the need to control others.

Roses — These are a symbol of prosperity and success in all areas of life, particularly romance.

Rudeness — If the dreamer is rude to someone in his dream, it shows that the dream concerns his relationship with his partner.

Ruler (for drawing lines) — This indicates the dreamer's need to be objective and honest when judging others, although in reality, this is not possible.

Running — This is a sign that during a trip in the near future, the dreamer will meet someone who will have a profound influence on his life.

Running Away/Fleeing — If the dreamer is running away from something, it means that a close friend is conspiring against him and joining forces with his enemies. If a person who is close to the dreamer is running away, it signifies that the dreamer's family will soon increase in size. An unsuccessful attempt to run away indicates that certain problems have not been solved.

Rust — This symbolizes disappointment in the realm of romance.

S

Saddle — This predicts travel or a trip accompanied by a surprise.

Sadness — A feeling of sadness and even depression actually means the exact opposite: The dreamer may expect a period filled with happiness and joy in the near future.

Safe (deposit box) — This symbolizes marriage. Breaking into a safe predicts that the dreamer will marry someone he has not yet met. An empty safe means an early marriage. A full safe indicates a late marriage.

Sage (the herb) — Dreaming about sage symbolizes the recovery from a serious disease, whether it is the dreamer's illness or that of someone close to him.

Sailing — This is symbolic of a good future and a variety of opportunities open to the dreamer.

Sailor — Dreaming about a sailor or seaman indicates sexual infidelity.

Saint — This indicates that the dreamer relies on a higher power for help.

Salad — Dreaming of preparing or eating a salad indicates that one of the dreamer's hidden talents will soon manifest itself and cover him with glory.

Salary — If a person dreams of receiving a raise, it is a warning about an upcoming incident.

Salmon — This symbolizes an obstacle that the dreamer will encounter, but one that he will eventually overcome through will power.

Salt — This is a very positive dream which heralds good luck and success in all areas of life.

Sand — This indicates conflicts and quarrels with family members.

Saw — If a male dreamer dreams that he is sawing something, it is a sign that he is reliable. If a woman saws something in a dream, it means that one of her friends will soon offer her helpful advice.

Scaffolding — This is a sign that an incorrect step taken by the dreamer may cause a lover's quarrel and even a break-up.

Scale (measuring) — This indicates an aspiration for justice and the ability to judge properly. Occasionally, a scale appearing in a dream suggests conjugal conflict.

Scar — This indicates the inability of the dreamer to break away from his past.

Scarf — Dreaming about a scarf is not a good sign. If the dreamer sees himself wrapped in a scarf, it means that he has a tendency toward depression. If a woman dreams about a scarf that bothers her when she wears it, it means that an intimate secret concerning her life will soon be revealed.

School — Dreaming about school indicates anxiety about failure. If the dreamer is an adult, the dream indicates frustration and a feeling of missed opportunities and failure. If the dreamer is a young person, it means that he is avoiding responsibility.

Scissors — A person close to the dreamer is pretending to be his friend; however, he is not.

Scratch — If the dreamer scratches another person, it is a sign that he has a very critical nature.

Scratching — This symbolizes unfounded concerns.

Screen — This indicates that the dreamer suffers from emotional problems.

Seagull — The seagull is a sign of bad news: the dreamer is likely to hear news that will cause him sadness and distress.

Search — Searching for something warns that the dreamer is acting in haste, not paying attention to important and meaningful details. The search for a person signifies fear of loss.

Seeds (to plant) — This means that the dreamer's elaborate plans for the future will indeed be realized.

Seeds — A dream about any kind of seed always signifies good things. The dreamer will find happiness and blessings through his efforts.

Selling — A dream about selling one's private property is a sign that the dreamer will have financial difficulties in the near future.

Separation — This means that the dreamer will have to make concessions in his life.

Servant — If the dreamer has a servant in the dream, it means that his standard of living will increase and he will be financially successful.

Sewage — Sewage in a dream is indicative of an unsuccessful marriage, of hidden enemies or of a bad business connection.

Shadows — Dreaming of shadows indicates that there will be a great improvement in economic status as well as significant monetary profits.

Shampooing (the hair) — This is an indication of gossip and revealed secrets.

Shark — This signifies that the dreamer unconsciously fears the dark.

Sheep — These show that it will be worthwhile for the dreamer to stick to his chosen path tenaciously.

Shell/Oyster — This means that good and positive

things are on their way: happiness, joy, financial and business success.

Shelter — Searching for a shelter means that the dreamer is very fearful of enemies. Building a shelter signifies the desire to escape from one's enemies.

Shelves — Empty shelves indicate that there will be losses and failures. Full shelves are a sign of great financial and material success.

Shepherd — This symbolizes the dreamer's hidden need to be involved in spiritual matters.

Ship — Dreaming about a ship is only meaningful if the ship's captain appears in the dream. If so, it indicates success in most areas of the dreamer's life.

Shooting — If someone shoots the dreamer, it means that he fears significant losses in the future.

Short (physique) — If the dreamer or one of his friends appears as a short person, it means that the dreamer will make progress in most areas of his life.

Shortage/Hunger — This predicts particularly good things and indicates a positive turnabout in the dreamer's life.

Shovel — Stoking a fire with a shovel indicates that the dreamer can expect good times.

Shower — This symbolizes the desire for sexuality and love. A dream about taking a shower with a partner indicates a good sex life.

Sigh — A dream in which the dreamer sighs is indicative of a good period, and means that the dreamer does not owe anyone anything.

Silk — If a woman dreams about silk, it symbolizes that she is happy with her family and love life. If the dreamer is a man, it is a sign that he will be highly successful in business.

Silverware — This represents a marriage in the family or of a close friend of the dreamer.

☆ Dream Interpretation ☆

Singing — If the dreamer or another person is singing, it is a prediction of a difficult period, full of obstacles and problems.

Skeleton — This is a sign that the dreamer's problems will all be solved soon.

Skin — If a dreamer sees his skin, it indicates a non-spiritual, materialistic personality.

Skull — This is a symbol of domestic problems.

Sky — This indicates a change for the better, accompanied by happiness and joy.

Sleep — If the dreamer sees himself sleeping, it warns of others who aim to harm him.

Smoke — Black smoke warns of possible problems in family life.

Smoking — This predicts an unfavorable period accompanied by frustration and anxiety.

Snail — This heralds good, joyous news, particularly news that is very touching.

Snake — A snake is a warning against falsehood. If one dreams about a snake bite, it means that someone close to him is lying to him and deceiving him. Killing a snake in a dream indicates the end of a friendship.

Snow — Any type of snow in a dream indicates extreme fatigue.

Soldier — This indicates that the dreamer is involved in conflicts or quarrels.

Son/Daughter — This represents the need for respect from others. A dream about a lost or sick son is a warning about the future.

Spider — In the context of European culture, the spider symbolizes a woman. The dream means that a woman will control the dreamer's life (even if the dreamer is a woman).

Spider-Web — A spider-web being woven around the dreamer means that the dreamer will achieve his objectives despite obstacles along the way.

Spools of Thread — These indicate unhappy feelings due to the dreamer's inability to cope with the tasks at hand.

Spoon/Teaspoon — Attests to a good and happy family life. Losing a spoon or teaspoon represents the dreamer's feeling that others are suspicious of him although he has done them no wrong.

Spy — If the dreamer sees himself as a spy, it predicts an unsuccessful adventure.

Squirrel — This predicts good times accompanied by success in all areas of life.

Stains — These indicate difficulties, frustrations and fears.

Statue — A statue is a sign of a self-imposed change in the dreamer's life.

Steer (animal) — This indicates the dreamer's honesty and fairness, which are his most outstanding character traits. If more than one steer appears in a dream, it shows that this is the right time to take risks (A steer, as opposed to a bull or cow, is characterized by his horns; see **Bull**.)

Store/Shop — If the dreamer is actually a storekeeper, it indicates business problems. If the dreamer does not own a shop, and he dreams that he is walking amongst the products on sale, it is a sign that he can expect good, pleasure-filled times.

Storeroom — A tidy storeroom is a sign of economic prosperity, pleasure and abundance. An empty storeroom is a warning against incorrect decisions, especially in the monetary sphere.

Stork — This symbolizes renewal and a change for the better in the dreamer's life.

Stranger — Dreaming about a stranger, especially one wearing a black suit, represents a warning about a bad period and depression in the life of the dreamer.

Straw — This reflects the dreamer's bad feelings. He sees his end and his destruction.

Struggle — Triumph over another person in a struggle is

a sign that the dreamer will overcome difficulties that stand in his way.

Suffering — Contrary to what might be expected, dreaming about pain or suffering is actually an indication of happiness, joy and laughter coming the way of the dreamer in the near future.

Suffocating/Choking — This expresses aggression and fear. If the dreamer is suffocating another person, it means that he feels hatred towards him. If the dreamer is being suffocated by another, it means that he deeply fears the person who is suffocating him in the dream.

Sugar — This symbolizes a good period in the dreamer's life accompanied by feelings of wholeness and harmony with his environment.

Suicide — This indicates the dreamer's desire to extricate himself from a difficult situation.

Suitcase — If the suitcase belongs to the dreamer, it indicates that he will soon have to deal with problems. If the suitcase belongs to someone else, it means that he will soon embark on a trip.

Sums (addition) — An incorrect sum warns against unsuccessful commercial negotiations.

Sunflower — This signifies sunshine, light and warmth.

Swan — This indicates a good family life. A black swan symbolizes a good and generous spouse; a white swan indicates a happy marriage and successful progeny.

Sweetness — A dream about eating something sweet means that the dreamer possesses a high level of inner awareness and self-control.

Swimming — If the dreamer sees himself swimming, it is a warning against taking unnecessary risks or gambling which will bring about significant losses.

T

Table — This symbolizes a person's accomplishments in life. A set table signifies a comfortable family life. A work table, operating table, desk, etc., are interpreted according to the context of their appearance in the dream.

Tailor — This is a sign that the dreamer is indecisive and easily influenced by others.

Tar — Tar on a road signifies good health. Tar on the soles of shoes or floating in water means that the dreamer will soon embark on a trip. Boiling tar means personal problems.

Taxi — If the dreamer sees himself hailing a taxi which then drives past him without stopping, it is a warning against being naive. If the dreamer hails a taxi uneventfully, he can expect a letter with good news in the near future.

Tea — This suggests that the dreamer could be more resolute in his opinions and more decisive in his manner.

Teacher — This indicates that the dreamer must examine his financial and social situation and act cautiously.

Tear — A tear indicates extreme emotional changes.

Tears — If tears are shed in a dream, it means that the dreamer will enjoy a rosy future and happy events.

Teeth — Dreaming about teeth or about a dentist warns of health problems. The dreamer should look after himself in the near future.

Telephone — If the dreamer is speaking on the telephone, he can expect success in the area under discussion. A ringing telephone in a dream means that a friend needs help. A silent telephone is symbolic of the fact that the dreamer feels discriminated against.

Telescope — This indicates possible changes in the dreamer's career or professional life.

Temptation — If the dreamer is being enticed by another person to perform a criminal act, the dream is a test and warning: Do not be tempted to walk forbidden paths in real life!

Tennis — This is a sign that the dreamer feels the need to be popular and socially successful.

Tent — This symbolizes protection and security. In the future, the dreamer will not face worry or disappointment.

Theater — This shows that the dreamer has a strong desire to break his routine and bring his talents and creativity to the fore.

Thigh — A thigh signifies recovery from a disease or the end of health problems.

Thimble — This is a symbol of unrealistic, unrealizable ambitions.

Thorn — This signifies that someone in the dreamer's environment is plotting against him and seeking to harm him.

Thread — A torn thread indicates disappointment or loss brought about by the compassionate character of the dreamer.

Ticket — Buying, receiving or handing someone a ticket indicates that a problem that has been bothering the dreamer lately will soon be solved.

Tin — This is a warning that deceitful people surround the dreamer.

Toad — The toad is a symbol of corruption. The dream warns against being tempted to engage in impure acts.

Toast — This is a sign of a successful and enjoyable family life.

Tobacco — Tobacco in any form, whether the dreamer or another person in the dream is smoking, indicates that the dreamer's problems will soon be solved, and that his character is conciliatory and moderate.

Tomato — The dreamer has a need for social involvement.

Torture — This expresses a vague fear or unbridled feelings of jealousy.

Tower — If the dreamer sees himself standing at the top of a high building, it means that he will suffer financial difficulties, but will have a life full of happiness. Climbing a tower in a dream indicates problems in business. Climbing down a rope from a tower means economic success and prosperity.

Toys — Clean, well-kept toys are a sign of happiness and joy for the dreamer. Broken toys signify difficult and sad times.

Trap — If the dreamer falls into a trap, it indicates that he is a suspicious type, suspicious even of those who do not deserve it. If the dreamer himself laid the trap, it is a sign that he will soon lose a court case.

Trees — Trees in bloom are a sign of a new love. Bare trees indicate marital problems.

Triangle — This shows that there is a conflict in the dreamer's mind, usually connected with choosing a marriage partner.

Trumpet — If a trumpet is heard in a dream, it signifies a change for the better. If the dreamer himself is playing the trumpet, it means he will succeed in overcoming difficulties that face him.

Tunnel — Driving through a tunnel signifies a lack of confidence. If the dreamer sees himself trapped in a tunnel, it means that he is trying to shirk responsibility.

Turtle — This predicts disappointment in one's love life.

Twins — This means that the dreamer will make a decision that will not bring about the anticipated results.

U

Ugliness — This signifies only good things for the dreamer.

Ulcer (stomach) — An ulcer is an indication of dissatisfaction as well as embarrassment which manifests itself in day-to-day life.

Umbrella — An open umbrella symbolizes happiness, success and love of life.

Unicorn — This mythical animal is connected to virginity and sexuality in the dreamer's life.

Uniform (clothing) — If a uniform appears in a dream (on condition that it is *not* the dreamer who is wearing it), it signifies that the dreamer has been blessed with peace, tranquillity and true love by the people around him.

University — This is a dream that bodes well: It indicates ambition and the desire for achievements, as well as a high level of success in all areas of life.

V

Vacation — This indicates that the dreamer's life is about to change for the better, becoming calmer and more peaceful.

Vagina — Dreaming about a vagina has a sexual interpretation which depends on the character of the dreamer.

Valley — This is a sign that there will be a change in place of residence.

Vampire — This signifies the dreamer's lack of self-confidence.

Vase — This indicates that the dreamer is egocentric and only cares about his own good, and that the dreamer must demonstrate a higher degree of empathy and sensitivity toward others.

Vegetables — Eating vegetables in a dream reflects the dreamer's careful nature: He does not like to take unnecessary risks.

Vegetation — Dreaming about green vegetation is a good sign: The dreamer can expect exciting surprises or good news.

Velvet — This signifies problems, arguments and domestic quarrels.

Victory — This is a warning against taking sides in an argument in which the dreamer has very little knowledge of the subject at hand.

Village — If the dreamer sees himself in an unknown village, there will be changes in his life in the near future.

Vine — A vine with grapes indicates hard work that will result in prosperity and great success.

Vinegar — This symbolizes jealousy, or that one of the dreamer's principal traits is jealousy which may make him suffer throughout his life.

Vineyard — This signifies success in the economic field and particularly in the field of romance.

Violence — This is an indication of pressure, anxiety or fear of the person or factor that the dreamer encounters in his dream.

Violets —These indicate a love of the good life, hedonism and the pursuit of pleasure.

Violin — If one hears a violin in a dream, it means the dreamer is becoming increasingly popular in social circles. If a violin string snaps, it signifies that the dreamer is a peace-maker. Tuning a violin indicates an imminent love affair.

Voices — Hearing voices in a dream (without seeing their source) means that the dreamer will soon experience feelings of distress, sadness or depression.

Volcano — The dreamer harbors an urgent need to control his emotions.

Vomiting — This reflects an uneasy conscience. The dreamer is tormented because his actions were not pure.

Vote — If the dreamer's vote is the deciding vote, it signifies a lack of confidence, a low self-image, and an impractical nature.

Voting — Voting with a ballot attests to the dreamer's need for social involvement and the desire to be influential.

Vow — This is a sign of an improvement in business and in one's financial situation.

Vulture — Dreaming about a vulture (or any bird of prey) is a sign that a cold and ruthless enemy threatens the dreamer.

W

Wages — Receiving wages in a dream indicates that without the dreamer's knowledge, someone is causing him harm and undermining him.

Waiter/Waitress — This shows that the dreamer has an ambitious personality, and is striving to improve his financial situation.

Waking — If the dreamer dreams that he is being awakened from sleep, a close and beloved person is about to appear and bring him much joy.

Walking — Walking along a long, unbroken path indicates that the dreamer must cope with problems in his life. A brisk, steady walk means that he will overcome all the obstacles along his way.

Wall — If the wall is solid and erect, the dream represents a warning against danger. If the wall is crumbling and falling, it actually symbolizes protection, and the dreamer will not be harmed.

Wallet — If the dreamer finds a wallet, it indicates prosperity and financial success. The loss of a wallet predicts disappointment and frustration.

Walnut — This is a sign of marriage to a rich partner. Eating walnuts in a dream indicates that the dreamer is wasteful and extravagant.

War — If the dreamer declares war, it signifies success in the areas of business and economics. If he is a witness to war, it means that he must avoid actions that might endanger him, and only act following careful consideration.

Wasp —If the dreamer sees a wasp, it means that bad news is on the way.

Water — Drinking clear water is a sign of success, happiness and abundance. Drinking impure water warns against health problems. Dreaming about playing in water signifies that the dreamer is given a lot of love by those around him. Stormy waters indicate problems on the path to economic independence.

Waterfall — This means that the great efforts that the dreamer has made will not bear fruit. If the dreamer sees another individual swimming under the waterfall, it means that the person is in danger.

Watermelon — This symbolizes superstition, and reflects hidden fears and concealed anxiety.

Wax — This warns against wastefulness and extravagance.

Wedding — Dreaming about a wedding usually expresses the dreamer's wish. When a bachelor dreams about his own wedding, it means that unpleasant news is on its way. If a bachelor dreams of another person's wedding, it means that a period of happiness awaits him. If a married person dreams about a stranger's wedding, it means that he is jealous of his spouse.

Whale — This is a sign that the dreamer is deprived of maternal love.

Wheat — This symbolizes abundance, success and material wealth.

Whistle — This means that ill-intentioned people are spreading malicious gossip about him.

Widowed — If a dreamer dreams about being widowed from his spouse, this ensures a long life for his partner. An unmarried person who dreams about being widowed may expect marriage in the future.

Wig — This is a sign of a lack of confidence in one's love life, and a struggle in making choices in romance.

Wildness/Raging — If the dreamer participates in a wild, unruly event causing him to panic, it predicts financial difficulties in the near future.

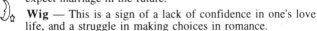

Will — Writing a will in a dream is actually a sign of a long and happy life.

Willow - Dreaming of a willow has a painful significance: Mistakes made in the family context cannot be rectified.

Wind — A strong wind, one that causes the dreamer anxiety, is a sign that he will find it difficult to cope with everyday life. If the strong wind does not frighten him, it shows that he will be able to cope with problems easily and successfully.

Window — If the dreamer is gazing out of a window, this means that he will be reconciled with someone with whom he has quarrelled. If another person is looking at the dreamer through a window, it warns of malicious gossip.

Wine — The interpretation of wine in a dream depends on the particular culture: Some interpret wine as a sign of abundance, while others see it as a symbol of drunkenness and failure. Usually it means that the dreamer can expect family celebrations.

Winter — Wintry weather indicates success in the near future. A dream about winter is sometimes interpreted as a sign of family problems, particularly parent-child relationships.

Witch — Bad news can be expected soon.

Wolf — The appearance of a wolf in any form in a dream signifies bad news. The news will be even more awful if the dream is about a pack of wolves.

Workshop — This indicates that the dreamer will be able to achieve all to which he aspires. Any task that he undertakes will be a success.

Worm — This means the same as a dream about a snake, but to a lesser degree. (See **Snake**.)

Writing — If the dreamer is writing a letter, it means that a letter will arrive. If others are writing a letter, the dreamer will quarrel with someone who is close to him.

X

X-ray — This signifies fear of poor health or serious financial problems.

Y

Yeast — This indicates a good life, abundance and a satisfying economic situation.

Z

Zebra — This signifies that the dreamer will suffer from a severe illness or fatal accident in the future.

Zodiac — This is a symbol of prosperity and economic and social success, following a great deal of effort and hard work.

Zoo — Visiting a zoo is a sign of a good and successful future.

East Yorkshire

Sally Burnard

COUNTRYSIDE BOOKS
NEWBURY BERKSHIRE

First published 2012
© Sally Burnard 2012

COUNTRYSIDE BOOKS
3 Catherine Road
Newbury, Berkshire

To view our complete range of books,
please visit us at
www.countrysidebooks.co.uk

ISBN 978 1 84674 280 4

Cover picture of Selwicks Bay, Flamborough Head
© Roy Rainford, via Robert Harding World Imagery

Designed by Peter Davies, Nautilus Design
Produced through MRM Associates Ltd., Reading
Typeset by Mac Style, Nafferton, East Yorkshire
Printed by Information Press, Oxford

Contents

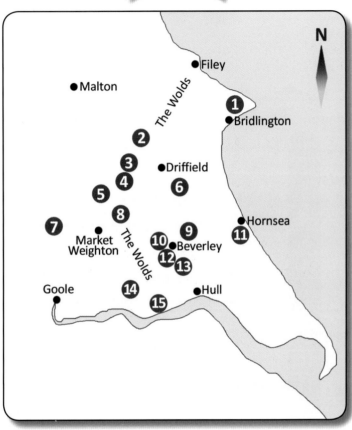

Area map showing location of the walks

Introduction

East Yorkshire is far less well known than its neighbours to the north and west whose wilder moors and dales regularly feature as a backdrop to film and TV dramas. By contrast, this is a gentler, more agricultural landscape but, nonetheless, full of variety for the walker.

Between the Vale of York to the west and the plain of Holderness to the east run the chalk hills of the Yorkshire Wolds with their airy uplands, wide skies and meandering, hidden valleys. Walkers can enjoy splendid views here on undulating terrain with only an occasional sharp climb. The book also includes walks on level terrain such as a rail trail, cliff top or river bank. In recent years, the council has replaced numerous stiles with kissing-gates in order to make its footpaths easier to use.

The pubs that have been chosen as starting points for the walks cater for a range of tastes and pockets (sometimes even within the same establishment). Walkers are given a friendly welcome, but please do remove any muddy footwear and check if you may use the car park whilst on a walk. Walking boots or sturdy trainers are recommended for all the routes.

I hope this book will bring you much pleasure. My thanks go to Norma Allin, Dawn Cowley, Les and Bill Eldridge, Ann Harper, Pat and Bob Heap, Mike Jackson, Stephen Greenfield, Jan Parr and Irene Wallace for their companionship, proof-reading and helpful suggestions during its preparation.

Thanks also to the volunteers of the East Yorkshire and Derwent Area of the Ramblers Association for their tireless work in monitoring, maintaining and improving the East Riding footpath network in conjunction with the East Riding of Yorkshire Council. If you come across problems such as a broken stile or an overgrown path, please inform the ERYC Countryside Access Team at County Hall, Beverley, HU17 9BA. ☎ 01482 395202 or 395204 or report online at www.eastriding.gov.uk/countrysideaccess.

Sally Burnard

Publisher's Note

We hope that you obtain considerable enjoyment from this book; great care has been taken in its preparation. However, changes of landlord and actual closures are sadly not uncommon. Likewise, although at the time of publication all routes followed public rights of way or permitted paths, diversion orders can be made and permissions withdrawn.

We cannot, of course, be held responsible for such diversion orders and any inaccuracies in the text which result from these or any other changes to the routes nor any damage which might result from walkers trespassing on private property. We are anxious though that all details covering the walks are kept up to date and would therefore welcome information from readers which would be relevant to future editions.

The simple sketch maps that accompany the walks in this book are based on notes made by the author whilst checking out the routes on the ground. However, for the benefit of a proper map, we do recommend that you purchase the relevant Ordnance Survey sheet covering your walk. The Ordnance Survey maps are widely available, especially through booksellers and local newsagents.

1 Sewerby

The Ship Inn

The quaint village of Sewerby is situated a mile up the coast from Bridlington. In summer it can be reached from Bridlington by taking the 'land train' which runs along the cliff top. The walk includes stretches of cliff-top paths with glorious views towards Flamborough and also explores Danes Dyke, a lovely, steep-sided wooded ravine running down to the sea. This section of the Yorkshire coast is notorious for its 'sea fret', a low, rolling mist which can take you by surprise when it comes in from the sea, causing a sudden, sharp drop in temperature even on a summer's day. Be prepared!

Distance – 2½ or 4½ miles.

OS Explorer 301 Scarborough, Bridlington & Flamborough Head GR TA202689.

Some steep ascents and descents mainly using steps, but these can be avoided by taking the short cut which keeps to fairly level ground.

Starting point The Ship Inn, Sewerby YO15 1EW.

How to get there *From Bridlington, take Sewerby Road, then the right fork when you reach the village. The Ship Inn is located at the eastern end of the village on the corner of two very narrow roads, Cliff Road and Church Lane.*

THE PUB The **Ship Inn** is set back from the sea with a south-facing paved beer garden and children's play area running down towards the cliff top. It is a traditional, family-friendly pub, serving reasonably priced, nicely-presented meals. There is a comfortable dining area/carvery. The Ship prides itself on its cask beers and tries to promote small, independent breweries with its guest beers.

Open 11 am to 11 pm every day.
☎ *01262 672374; www.shipinnsewerby.co.uk*

1 From the front of the pub, turn immediately right onto a paved footpath between two wire fences with the sea over to your right. Carry on to a footpath sign and turn right, making your way towards the cliff edge.

2 As you approach the cliff edge, leave the paved path which goes towards **Bridlington** and turn left along the grassy cliff top beside the cricket field. The white cliffs of **Flamborough Head** come into sight ahead of you. At the end of the sports ground, continue in the same easterly direction on a clear track along the cliff edge. You will pass a redundant kissing-gate. There are good views back towards Bridlington bay. The cliffs are subject to erosion, so do not stray too close to the edge.

3 After a mile or so, you will see the trees of **Danes Dyke** ahead of you. If the tide is low enough, a small beach is visible. As you approach it, turn sharp left away from the eroded cliff edge for about 50 yards to a path junction* then take the path which descends steeply towards the beach keeping the steep ravine to your left.

For the shorter, level walk, do not take the beach path at the junction but bear left along the top of the ravine for about 200 yards enjoying the lovely view below. Keep on this path until you reach the path junction at point 11 and then turn left.

4 **Main route:** Go up the stone steps on the far side of the beach to rejoin the cliff path. Continue on stone steps up to the top, ignoring a dirt track to the right. At the top, bear right and follow the footpath indicated towards **South Landing** and **Flamborough Head**.

5 **Beacon Hill**, the highest point of the walk, comes into sight ahead. Before you reach it, the path descends into a little gully and back up to a stony track on the other side.

6 At the top of the hill, turn left at the footpath junction, taking the route indicated towards **Flamborough** and head inland. This path winds its way towards the outskirts of Flamborough village, eventually passing over a stile by a little gate. Go over the next stile by a metal gate, passing a campsite on your left and converted farm buildings to the right.

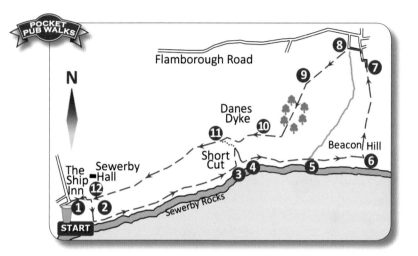

Flamborough Road

N

Danes
Dyke

Short
Cut

Beacon Hill

The
Ship
Inn

Sewerby
Hall

Sewerby Rocks

START

7 Continue in the same northerly direction on the road ahead. When you reach a T-junction, turn left in front of a long, low, white house, then follow the road round to the right, and take the second road on the left, **Water Lane**, just before the cemetery.

8 When the road bears right, take the footpath going off diagonally to your left between wire fences alongside animal enclosures. Continue past some wooden gates into the next field and follow the wire fence along the bottom edge.

9 At the end of the wire fence, turn left and pass through a metal kissing-gate onto a permissive path leading through a belt of trees. It is waymarked to **Danes Dyke** car park and toilets. Bear right on the main track as the wood narrows.

10 Cross over a gap between two fields and carry on into light woodland. Look out for a signpost to the right indicating steps leading downwards. Go down and cross the bridge to the other side of the ravine. You will emerge into the Danes Dyke car park with a small café and toilets opposite.

Turn immediately right past an information board and take the chalky path alongside the road out of the car park. When the road divides, cross over and take the path on the left signposted Headland Way and Sewerby Village. This takes you down a very long flight of steps into a deep, fern-filled gorge. Cross the bridge at the bottom and turn left. At a fork, bear right going up a gentler incline with steps. Bear left onto the footpath to the beach and **Sewerby** village. The path descends to another junction after a few more steps.

11 Bear right here and shortly afterwards cross over a chalky track. Continue on a narrow dirt path. From here you will have sea views to the left. Keep on along this narrow path, passing a gap to the golf course on your right, derelict farm buildings and then the clubhouse. The tower of **Bridlington church** comes into view ahead. After passing a concrete bunker/pillbox on the left, you will eventually reach the cricket field. Go straight ahead with the pavilion to your left. On the right, the imposing façade of **Sewerby Hall** comes into view.

12 You will pass an information board on a kiosk at one of the entrances to Sewerby Hall. To return to the pub, go straight ahead at the next footpath junction and down a little dip skirting the animal enclosure to rejoin the path to the village.

Place of interest nearby

Sewerby Hall, almost adjacent to the start of the walk, houses memorabilia of Amy Johnson and her record-breaking flights in the 1930s. There is also a small zoo, pleasant gardens to explore and a tea room. ☎ 01262 673769; www.eastriding.gov.uk/sewerby/

The Triton Inn

The attractive estate village of Sledmere is situated in lovely, rolling countryside. Sledmere House is a fine, 18th-century Georgian house set in a 'Capability' Brown inspired landscape. The elegant house and parkland has been the seat of the Sykes family for over 200 years. Previous generations of the family made an impact on the landscape by planting hundreds of acres of new woodland and pioneering agricultural improvements. They were also responsible for the restoration of many of the local churches in the Victorian era. The walk goes through the village then follows part of the perimeter of the grounds of Sledmere House on a woodland path, and continues through the deer park.

Distance – 3 miles.

OS Explorer 300 Howardian Hills & Malton GR SE933648.

Good tracks and grassy paths. There are three 7-ft-high ladder stiles along the route so you will need to be reasonably nimble to negotiate these. Please note that most of the walk is on permissive paths on the estate which may occasionally be closed when special events are taking place so do please check with the East Riding of Yorkshire Council's Rights of Way Department before setting off. ☎ 01482 395321.

Starting point The Triton Inn, Sledmere YO25 3XQ.

How to get there Sledmere is 7 miles north-west of Driffield on the B1253 road between Bridlington and Malton. It can also be reached from the A166 via the B1251 from Fridaythorpe or the B1252 from Garton on the Wolds. The Triton Inn is situated on the main village street at the junction with the Luttons road. Car parking is available to the side and rear of the pub and also by the green near the Eleanor Cross on the main street of the village. There are also some parking spaces opposite the former Methodist chapel at the eastern end of the village. If you park here you can cut out about ½ mile of road walking through the village.

THE PUB

The **Triton Inn** is a quintessential country inn which is leased by the current proprietors from the Sledmere Estate and is situated a few hundred yards from the entrance to Sledmere House. The comfortable interior is traditional in style, with beams, brasses and open fires. The menu is wide-ranging and includes some classic, reasonably-priced pub fare, as well as more expensive choices. Visitors are given a friendly welcome and hot meals are served with generous portions of seasonal vegetables. It can be very busy at weekends.

It is open from 12 noon to 3 pm and 6 pm to midnight on Monday to Saturday (closed Monday lunchtime in winter); 12 noon to 9.30 pm on Sunday. ☎ *01377 236078; www.thetritoninn.co.uk*

1 On leaving the pub car park, turn right along the main road which takes you down through the village, passing a pair of gate lodges to the estate on the right, then the Bridlington road junction, the school and the former Methodist chapel on your left. You will then pass a small gate into the grounds of **Sledmere House** on your right. Do not enter, but continue straight ahead along the south-west side of the road on an attractive mown grass path

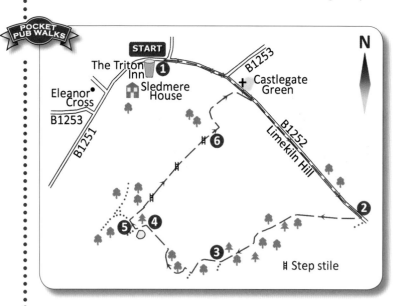

bordered by daffodils in the spring. The route goes gradually uphill (**Limekiln Hill**).

2 At the brow of the hill, turn right into a wooded area and follow the path westwards with pleasant views across **Sledmere Park** below you to the right. Keep following yellow waymarks, disregarding an entrance to the park on your right and a left fork.

3 After about ½ mile, at a second fork, keep bearing right. The route is clearly waymarked and affords a good open view across the park to **Sledmere House** itself. The track turns right and follows the fence. A large deer shed comes into view ahead and the route turns sharp right alongside the high deer fence. The route circles round the left-hand side of a small copse then continues downhill.

4 Bear left round a pond to your left, then right. Continue downhill, looking for a waymark indicating the route through the trees to your right about halfway down to the valley bottom.

Looking across the parkland to Sledmere House

At this point, it is worth a short detour down to the valley and then along to the left to see the interesting memorial stone marking the graves of family pets on which is inscribed a moving poem by Byron. You find the monument on your right. Retrace your steps to the path junction and bear up to the right, ignoring the well-defined track straight ahead of you. About halfway back up to the pond, turn left onto the waymarked route through the trees at point 5.

5 The path leads through the trees and continues in the same north-easterly direction across parkland (it may be indistinct to begin with). You will need to negotiate three tall ladder stiles in the deer fencing. After the second of these, there is an excellent view of the house to your left beyond a ha-ha. After the second ladder stile, the route heads towards some farm buildings.

6 Climb the last ladder stile which is located to the left of these buildings. Continue right up to a fence, then turn left along a grassy track (permissive path) next to the fence. Keep following the fence, eventually going past a brick building, then back to the fence which bears right to rejoin the main road through the village. Turn left along the road to return to the **Triton Inn.**

Place of interest nearby

A visit to **Sledmere House**, with its 18th-century furnishings and spectacular Turkish room is highly recommended. There is a café, gift shop and plant stalls. There is also a small art gallery housed in part of the old model farm buildings on the opposite side of the road. ☎ 01377 236637; http://sledmerehouse.com

3 Wetwang

The Black Swan

This walk provides glorious views of the surrounding countryside without having to climb any significant hills. Near the start of the route you can enjoy a view of the distinctive rocket-shaped, 120-ft-high, Sir Tatton Sykes monument on the skyline ahead. The land-owning Sykes family of nearby Sledmere House were responsible in large part for significant agricultural development in the Yorkshire Wolds. You will also pass an interesting wildlife area and be able to stride out along an ancient green lane formerly used as a drove road. The late Richard Whiteley, presenter of *Countdown*, was famously mayor of this village.

Distance – 5¼ or 6½ miles.

OS Explorer 294 Market Weighton & Yorkshire Wolds Central and 300 Howardian Hills & Malton. GR SE934592.

Field paths and farm tracks.

Starting point The Black Swan, Wetwang YO25 9XJ.

How to get there Wetwang is conveniently situated on the A166 York to Bridlington road, about 5 miles west of Driffield. The Black Swan is on the north side of the A166 at the eastern end of the village by the junction with the minor road to Sledmere, just opposite the village pond. Street parking is available off the main road near the church.

THE PUB

The **Black Swan** has a car park to the side and a long grassed area to the rear with a beer garden and children's playground. Generous portions of traditional pub food are served in the homely interior. Sadly, the black swans after whom the pub is named are no longer to be seen on the adjacent village pond.

Open Monday, Tuesday, Thursday, and Friday from 12 noon to 2 pm and from 5 pm till late; Wednesday from 5 pm; Saturday and Sunday from 12 noon to late. ☎ 01377 23602.

1 On leaving the pub, turn immediately left by the village pond onto **Station Hill**. About 50 yards down the road, look for a footpath sign on the right, opposite **Northfield Road**. Take the path which passes through a children's play area.

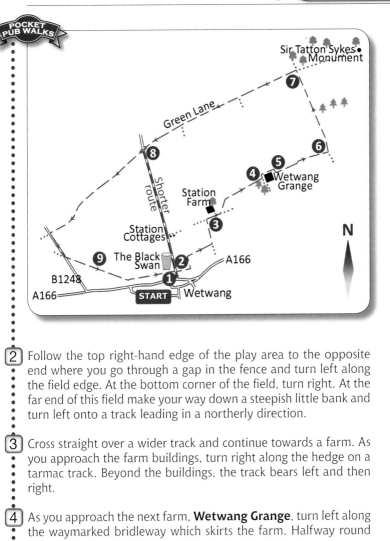

[2] Follow the top right-hand edge of the play area to the opposite end where you go through a gap in the fence and turn left along the field edge. At the bottom corner of the field, turn right. At the far end of this field make your way down a steepish little bank and turn left onto a track leading in a northerly direction.

[3] Cross straight over a wider track and continue towards a farm. As you approach the farm buildings, turn right along the hedge on a tarmac track. Beyond the buildings, the track bears left and then right.

[4] As you approach the next farm, **Wetwang Grange**, turn left along the waymarked bridleway which skirts the farm. Halfway round

the north side of the farm another waymarked track bears uphill to your left. Ignore this (unless you wish to shorten the walk) and continue skirting the farm buildings.

5️⃣ Turn left along the bottom of the field. A wildlife area has been established along the southern side of this field where different species of wild flowers abound – a delightful sight, especially in early to mid-summer when it attracts a variety of butterflies on warm, sunny days.

Continue in an easterly direction along the bottom edge of the field. At the end of the field, the route bears left, then immediately right, to continue along the edge of the next field. Two smallish wind turbines come into view ahead.

6️⃣ The field edge path dips down, then up to meet a chalky track where you turn left, heading up towards the woods. When this track bears sharply to the right, continue straight ahead towards a metal gate, then up the track beyond with trees on your left. Go past the wood on your left and continue steadily uphill to a metal gate and T-junction with a wide track (another grassy track continues opposite). This is an excellent place to pause and admire the view behind you.

The Sir Tatton Sykes monument

7️⃣ Turn left onto the wide track (unless you wish to detour to the monument which is about

½ mile up to the right). Follow the wide, grassy track for about 1½ miles until you reach a minor road. Down to your left are vestiges of an old station on the Driffield to Malton line. Railway enthusiasts are currently attempting to resuscitate a part of this route known as the Malton Dodger.

At this point you can turn left to return to the village by the shorter route along the minor road. There are good verges to walk on until the last 70 yards or so.

8 Cross over the minor road and continue in the same westerly direction for about ¾ mile until you reach the main road. Turn left along the verge until you reach a broken stile and signpost on your left indicating a route heading diagonally uphill across the field towards the outskirts of the village. Head for the last house on the right until you reach a stile about 100 yards from the far corner of the field.

9 Go over the stile and continue diagonally uphill across a field of rough pasture. Pass through a small wooden gate to the right-hand side of black corrugated buildings then through a metal gate onto a minor road. To return to the pub, go straight ahead along this minor road at the back of the village to **Station Hill** where you turn right.

Place of interest nearby

In nearby Hull, there is the **Hull and East Riding Museum** which illuminates the rich archaeological heritage of the area. ☎ 01482 613902.

4 Millington

The Gait Inn

The tiny village of Millington nestles in the heart of the Yorkshire Wolds and its unique scenery attracts walkers from far and wide. This walk climbs gradually up out of Millington, then drops down to the junction of two dales. It then follows a winding route along a pretty valley up towards the head of Given Dale, one of the most picturesque spots in the Wolds.

Distance – 6 miles.

OS Explorer 294 Market Weighton & Yorkshire Wolds Central GR SE832518.

Minor roads, tracks and field paths, which can sometimes be muddy underfoot.

Starting point The Gait Inn, Millington YO42 1TX.

How to get there Millington is situated approximately 3 miles north-east of Pocklington and is reached via a turn-off on the minor road from Pocklington to Huggate. The Gait Inn is on the main street in the village. Alternate parking is available on the wide verges of Swineridge Lane, to the west of the village near the church.

THE PUB The **Gait Inn** is a friendly and unpretentious country pub, popular with locals and visitors alike. The building dates from the 16th century and has a homely, beamed interior. There is a large car park and a pleasant grassed beer garden to the rear. The menu features hearty portions of good, country fare.

Opening times are 12 noon to 3 pm and 6.30 pm till closing time on Friday, Saturday and Sunday. It is closed all day on Monday and open from 6.30 pm on Tuesday, Wednesday and Thursday; ☎ *01759 302045.*

1 From the front of the pub, turn left along the main street, then left again at the first side road. Go uphill passing the church on your right. When you reach the T-junction, turn right. Shortly afterwards, at the next road junction, turn left and go uphill on a minor road (**The Balk**).

2 At the next T-junction near the brow of the hill, cross over and take the bridleway bearing slightly right then descending gradually to **Little Givendale Farm**. Make your way through the farm following yellow waymarks.

3 The route then proceeds along the left-hand side of a field and uphill to a path junction. Take the direction indicated to the left and make your way down a steep slope to a bridge over **Whitekeld Beck**.

4 Go over the bridge and continue straight ahead on the path in the valley which eventually goes up through a gate and alongside a plantation of trees. After approximately ½ mile, the path bears to the right and a tiny church comes into view overlooking the valley and fishponds to your left.

5 Take the footpath from the churchyard up to the minor road and turn left. After 200 yards, go over a stile on your right at the end of the trees and take the footpath along the left-hand side of the plantation. After 300 yards take a left turn, up into a large field.

6 Follow the path down to the right along the field edge. Bear left round the bottom end contouring the hillside. Bear left again and go uphill along the opposite side of the field. After 200 yards take a waymarked path to the right.

7 Follow the narrow and often rather slippery path between barbed wire fences. At the end of the path, go over a footbridge and bear right then left alongside a wood on your right. After walking along the edge for 500 yards, the path bears to the left. Now look out for a waymarked path on your right which enters the wood.

8 Turn right into the wood and follow the path down to the bottom edge where you pass over a stile into a field. The route goes straight ahead across the field, bearing slightly left towards a stile in the opposite hedge and fingerpost beyond.

POCKET PUB WALKS

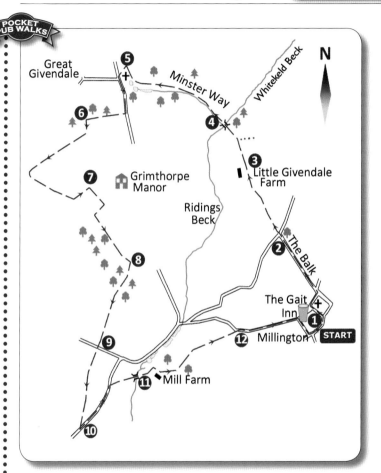

9. Go over the stile, cross the road, pass through a gap in the opposite hedge indicated by two fingerposts and continue heading in the same direction across a large field. The route continues into the next field through a gap near the right-hand corner of the hedge. After

passing farm buildings to your right, the path gets gradually closer to the minor road to the left. As you start to come level with a wind turbine over to your left, the field narrows and the path curves round to the left and leads to a gap in the hedge. Take care as you emerge onto the road as it can be unexpectedly busy at times.

10 Cross the road and turn left along the opposite verge heading back towards the distant hills. After about 300 yards you will reach a stile on your right which takes you into a field of rough pasture. Head down through this field and bear slightly left towards the left-hand side of the farm buildings in the distance.

11 After passing under overhead wires, cross a footbridge over the wide stream at the bottom of the field. Go through a kissing-gate and turn left alongside a wire fence. The route goes over a stile by a metal gate, passing farm buildings to the right. Shortly afterwards, pass through a kissing-gate and turn right onto the farm track. As you draw level with the farm buildings, look out for a waymarked path on your left and make your way up a steep bank. Bear right along the field edge, then left alongside a plantation to join a track which emerges onto **Swineridge Lane**.

12 Turn right along the road, then take the first right turn to the centre of the village. Turn left to return to the pub.

Place of interest nearby

A visit to the scenic dale of **Millington Pastures** to the north-west of Millington is highly recommended. Take the minor road, Wood Gate, going in a northerly direction from the village to Millington Wood car park. You will have to negotiate a very narrow road and hairpin bends if you go by car.

The Wolds Inn

Huggate is set amidst stunning scenery and is the highest village in the Yorkshire Wolds. This delightful walk takes you to Horse Dale, one of the most impressive of the steep-sided dry valleys of the Yorkshire Wolds. It runs along a section of the ancient earthworks which once surrounded the Huggate area and offers superb views of the winding dale below.

East Yorkshire

Distance – 4 miles.

OS Explorer 294 Market Weighton & Yorkshire Wolds Central GR SE884550.

Tracks and field paths, as well as some grassland which can be rough in parts.

Starting point The Wolds Inn, Huggate YO42 1YH.

How to get there *Huggate is approximately 3 miles south of Fridaythorpe, and can be reached by a minor road off the A166 midway between York and Bridlington. The Wolds Inn is situated at the eastern end of the village on the road to Driffield. Parking in the village is very restricted due to the very narrow roads with steep banks. If not using the pub car park, you can park just to the west of the route of the walk on the wide verges of the Huggate to York road (York Lane) near the point where it is crossed by the Wolds Way (GR SE867557). From here, take the bridleway heading east and join the route at point 4.*

THE PUB The **Wolds Inn** is an inviting, wood-panelled, coaching inn dating back to the 16th century. Walkers and cyclists receive a friendly welcome here and portion sizes are legendary! There is a beer garden to the rear and a large car park.

Opening times are 12 noon to 2 pm and from 6 pm on Tuesday to Saturday; from 12 noon on Sunday. Closed all day Monday. ☎ *01377 288217; www.woldsinn.co.uk*

1 From the front of the pub, turn right along the road towards the centre of the village. Take the first turning on the right and head downhill, passing the village green on your right. At 300 ft, the well on the green is reputed to be one of the deepest in the country. Continue

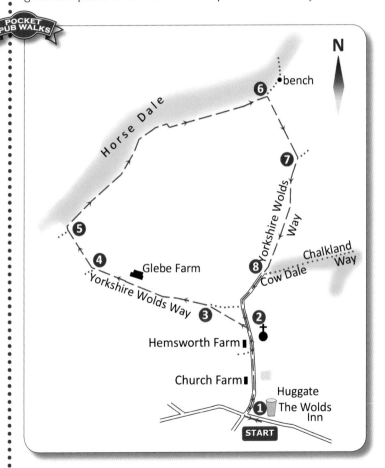

POCKET PUB WALKS

N

Horse Dale

bench 6

7

Yorkshire Wolds Way

5

Chalkland Way

4

Glebe Farm

Yorkshire Wolds Way 3

8

Cow Dale

2 ✝

Hemsworth Farm ■

Church Farm ■

Huggate
The Wolds
Inn

1

START

down the hill, passing the church on your right. In early spring, snowdrops abound in the churchyard.

2 Cross over and, after passing the last house on the left, just before the road starts to go steeply downhill, go through a kissing-gate on your left next to a metal gate. This leads you into a field of rough

Horse Dale (courtesy of Ray Wallis)

pasture. Take a diagonal route across the field, bearing downhill towards the opposite bottom corner. An indistinct green path passes through some interesting mounds and bumps.

3 Turn left at the bottom onto a surfaced farm track leading up towards **Glebe Farm** on the hillside ahead and to the right. Leave the farm track when it begins to bear right and continue on the narrow **Yorkshire Wolds Way** path between a hedge and a wire fence. When this path emerges onto a wide grass verge, carry on up to the fingerpost which you can see at the brow of the hill.

4 At the footpath junction, turn right along the right-hand side of a field. Go over the brow of the hill and pass through a wooden gate into the access area of **Horse Dale**. Although no public right of way is indicated to the right, this steep-sided dale is designated access land where walkers are free to roam.

5 Turn right onto a well-trodden grassy path which contours the top edge of the valley. The bank up to your right is part of the substantial earthworks which used to surround the whole of the Huggate area. Continue along the top of the dale for about a mile, passing a large gap in the hedge up to your right and then skirting round the bottom edge of a small plantation. Carry on round the top of the dale just

beneath the tree-line, enjoying splendid views of the winding valley below. Possibly on a very clear day you may even get a glimpse of the sea on the far horizon. Almost at the end of the small plantation, you will need to step over the single wire of a low, electric fence. Although clearly defined, the path can be uneven in places.

6) About 100 yards before you see an unusual wooden bench inscribed with lines of poetry, look out for a narrow path going steeply uphill to a footpath sign and a single tree in the hedge to your right. If you reach the bench, you have overshot the turning, so retrace your steps and the path up to the hedge will be more easily visible. Pass through a wooden gate and continue up the left-hand side of the hedge following the **Yorkshire Wolds Way** as indicated by the fingerpost.

7) At the far end of the field, turn right onto a surfaced track bordered by somewhat windswept cherry trees. The distinctive spire of **Huggate church** is visible in the distance. As you approach the village, the track goes downhill passing the entrance to another pretty valley to your left.

8) After the dip, the track climbs up towards the village centre, at first steeply, then more gently. Retrace your steps past the church and the village green on your left, then turn left onto the main road at the top of the hill to return to the pub.

Place of interest nearby

Bishop Wilton, approximately 5 miles to the west, via the A166, is a picturesque village at the foot of the Wolds, dissected by a stream. As its name suggests, it was once the site of an archbishop's palace. The church has an outstanding carved Norman doorway.

The White Horse Inn

Hutton and Cranswick were formerly two distinct villages but now belong to the same parish. This intriguing walk explores the village and its immediate surroundings. Those who are only familiar with the village as seen from the main road will find the walk surprisingly full of interest.

Hutton Cranswick Walk 6

Distance – 4 miles.

OS Explorer 295 Bridlington, Driffield & Hornsea GR TA025524.

Level and well-maintained paths. Care should be exercised at the two railway crossings.

Starting point The White Horse Inn, Hutton Cranswick YO25 9QN.

How to get there *Hutton Cranswick is situated on the A164 Beverley to Driffield road approximately 4 miles south of Driffield. The White Horse Inn is situated on the north side of the vast green at the southern end of the village, just opposite the duck pond. On-street parking is available for those not visiting the pub.*

THE PUB

The **White Horse Inn** is a modest and friendly establishment which has outlived the other pubs which used to serve the local residents. To the rear there is a grass beer garden, large car park and a camping area. Food is only served from 6 pm to 8 pm in the evenings, but cyclists and walkers who use the bar during the day are welcome to eat their own sandwiches in the pub's food lounge. Groups are welcome and tea and coffee are served.

The pub is open from 12 noon every day.
☎ *01377 270383; www.whitehorse.me.uk*

1 From the front of the pub, turn right, then immediately right onto the path which passes through the car park. Continue heading north on a grassy track to the right-hand side of the bowling club through an area of bramble patches. The path then goes left over

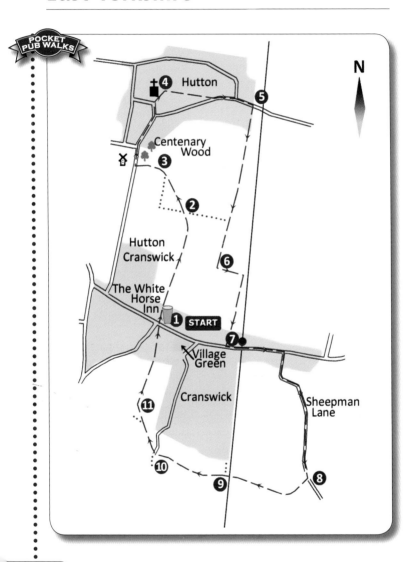

POCKET
PUB WALKS

N

4 Hutton

5

Centenary
Wood

3

2

Hutton
Cranswick

6

The White
Horse
Inn

1 START

7

Village
Green

11

Cranswick

Sheepman
Lane

10

9

8

a wooden footbridge. Go through a metal kissing-gate, then bear right along a well-trodden path towards a wooden kissing-gate on the opposite side of the field. Pass through the gate, continue along the path on the left-hand side of the next field and pass through another kissing-gate.

2. Continue round or across the next field heading towards the church tower beyond the top left-hand corner. When you reach the next kissing-gate you will see ahead of you an area of old chalk pits now grassed over and providing excellent toboggan runs in winter.

3. You now bear left to enter **Centenary Wood**, planted in 1996 to celebrate 100 years of the Parish Council and to provide a haven for wildlife. After entering the wood, bear left at the fork in the path. When you reach the far side of the wood, you will emerge onto a road via the access point near a large information board. Turn right along the road. When you reach the fork, bear left towards the churchyard. Enter the churchyard and follow the path, bearing right around the eastern end of the church.

4. The route leaves the churchyard via a metal kissing-gate on the right-hand side which leads to a tree-lined path heading east. The path emerges onto **Howl Lane** where you turn left and continue downhill for about 300 yards until you almost reach the railway line.

5. About 100 yards before the level crossing, look out for a fingerpost on the right and take the narrow, grassy footpath heading south. The path eventually takes you over a footbridge and a sturdy stile and continues in the same direction through rough pasture along the right-hand edge of the next field.

6. At the end of this long field, turn left and just before you reach the south-east corner of the field close to the railway, pass through a

wooden kissing-gate on your right and continue on a narrow grassy path. Near the entrance to an industrial unit on the right, the path reaches a T-junction where you turn left onto the road.

The delightful loco that stands on the station platform.

7 Cross the level crossing with care and carry on for about 200 yards and then take the road to the right, **Sheepman Lane**. The road bears left, then right, as you reach the fields. It now becomes a quiet lane with a stream on the left. The lane becomes a cinder track continuing in the same southerly direction. After passing a paddock on the right, as the track bears left, look out for a waymarked but unobtrusive footpath on your right.

8 Turn right onto this path which meanders left, then right between two fields and then goes right over a stream bed, as if to head back towards the village. After about 20 yards, however, turn left over a double footbridge over a stream. The path then takes you round the edge of the next field to a kissing-gate which brings you to the railway line.

9 Stop, look and listen before proceeding with caution to cross the line to the kissing-gate on the far side of the track. Ignore the footbridge to your right and carry on straight ahead along the right-hand edge of a field in a westerly direction. Continue on a tree-lined path which brings you to a house and a footpath junction.

10 At this junction, turn right towards **Cranswick**, but then turn almost immediately left after about 20 yards onto the public footpath. Pass through a metal gate (or over a stile) and take the diagonal route bearing ahead and to the right. When you almost reach a metal gate in a wooden fence, turn off to the right over a stile.

11 The route leads through a thick hedge and over a stream, then up into a field on the far side. Follow the field edge path to the left then go over (or past) a stile and turn immediately right onto a very narrow path between a hedge and a wire fence. Follow this path in a northerly direction until it emerges on the road opposite the village green.

Before returning to the pub, head across the green towards the red telephone box. Just before you reach it, you will see the millennium sun clock on the ground to your left. If the sun is shining, when you stand on the stone indicating the current month of the year, your shadow will point to the correct time. From here, make your way back to the pub via the pretty village duck pond.

Places of interest nearby

In Watton, approximately 2 miles to the south, off the A164, are the remains of **Watton Priory**. The beautiful Tudor brick house, now known at Watton Abbey, was formerly the prior's dwelling. The church is built in the same unusual style.

Top Hill Low Nature Reserve, signposted from the A164 at Watton, is a Site of Special Scientific Interest (SSSI) due to the richness of wildlife, particularly birds, that flourishes in and around the reservoirs.

The Plough Inn

This very pleasant walk takes you through the peaceful countryside of the Vale of York to the woods and sandy trails of Allerthorpe Common. Part of the common is a nature reserve and is reputed to be the best place in Britain to see adders, but do not let that put you off as they are very shy creatures. The common is a particularly delightful sight in late summer when the heather is in bloom. It is an open access area where you have freedom to roam off the paths within the boundaries shown on the OS Explorer map.

Distance – 5 miles.

OS Explorer 294 Market Weighton & Yorkshire Wolds Central GR SE782475.

Level terrain; good paths and tracks.

Starting point The Plough Inn, Allerthorpe YO42 4RW.

How to get there *Allerthorpe is situated in the Vale of York, just off the A1079 to the south-west of Pocklington between York and Market Weighton. The Plough is located at the bend on the main road. Parking is also available at Allerthorpe Common on the route of the walk.*

The **Plough Inn** is an attractive and popular pub, with friendly service, nicely-presented food and an interesting daily specials board. The home-cooked food uses local produce and there is a wide range of real ales.

Opening times are 12 noon to 3 pm and 5.30 pm to 11 pm Monday to Friday; 12 noon to 11 pm on Saturday; and 12 noon to 10.30 pm on Sunday. ☎ *01759 302349; www.ploughinnpub.co.uk*

 From the front of the pub, go to the right and turn immediately right onto the signposted track which runs beside the building in a northerly direction from the bend in the road. After about 250 yards, the track bears left and heads in a westerly direction, passing farm buildings on the left.

 Shortly afterwards the track forks. Bear left and continue in a westerly direction. The track leads over a small bridge and carries on towards woodland. It then passes alongside a large field. Just

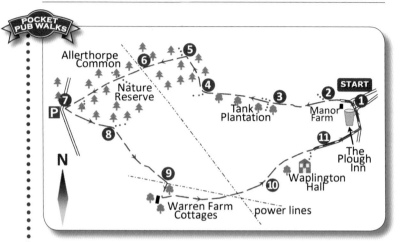

after the end of this field, look out for an opening on the left which takes you onto a bridleway in the woods on your left continuing in the same westerly direction.

3. After about 600 yards you will reach a wooden gate. Go through it into the woods beyond. Go straight ahead on the main track ignoring the little path to the right. Very shortly you will reach a slight clearing.

4. At the fork in the clearing, take the track bearing right. (Ignore the bridleway which goes off to the left.) The track continues in an almost northerly direction along the edge of the wood, becoming sandy and lined with heather and with a new plantation to the right.

5. At a double wooden fence and gate, turn left onto a grassy track leading in a westerly direction. Ahead you will see overhead wires crossing the track. When you reach the path junction below the wires, turn left if you wish to visit the nature reserve. A wooden gate and stile on your right lead into a cleared, heathery area.

6. After exploring the nature reserve, return to the path crossroads and continue in the same westerly direction as before. After

about ½ mile, the wide track eventually leads towards a minor road ahead, with a car park to your right.

7 Turn left onto the perimeter path close to the edge of the wood. This path meanders along between tall pines and bracken heading south-east.

8 After about 500 yards, go through a wooden gate on your right. Do not take the waymarked route to the right but continue straight ahead on a wide dirt track heading away from the wood in a south-easterly direction.

9 After the third field, turn right at the T-junction towards farm buildings. The route turns sharp left as you approach the farm onto a wide track heading east. You will pass a field of turf on your right and pass under a row of pylons.

10 After the next field the track enters a wooded area. Across a paddock on the left is a pleasant view of the Yorkshire Wolds. You will pass the buildings of **Waplington Hall** and a walled garden on the right. After a stream and pond on the right, a golf course comes into view.

11 The track becomes surfaced, heading towards the road ahead. When you reach the road, turn left along the main road to return to the pub.

Place of interest nearby

Allerthorpe Lakeland Park, ½ mile south of the village, offers a variety of water sports, including boat hire, fly fishing, as well as a campsite and children's play area. The café overlooking the lake is open from 10 am, Wednesday to Sunday. ☎ 01759 301444; www.allerthorpelakelandpark.co.uk

The Goodmanham Arms

This pleasant walk takes you along an undulating section
of the Yorkshire Wolds Way. A very gradual climb gives you
glorious views over the Vale of York to the west. The longer
route continues through Londesborough Park, an example of the
naturalistic style of 18th-century landscape gardening. The return
uses the Yorkshire Wolds Way and field edge paths.

Distance – 3 or 5 miles.

OS Explorer 294 Market Weighton & Yorkshire Wolds Central GR SE888431.

Most of the walk is on good tracks, but part of the Londesborough section includes some open pasture where the route is not well trodden.

Starting point The Goodmanham Arms, Goodmanham YO43 3JA.

How to get there *Goodmanham is approximately 1½ miles north-east of Market Weighton. From Market Weighton High Street, take Londesborough Road and after ½ mile turn right onto Goodmanham Road. Continue for ¾ mile to the village centre. The pub is on the right-hand side near the bend in the road before you reach the church. For those not visiting the pub, there is a good car park on the left-hand side of the main road at the southern end of Goodmanham.*

THE PUB

The **Goodmanham Arms** is a traditional village pub, with a small and cosy interior. Décor is eclectic and includes interesting items (some donated by local people) which will bring back memories to customers of a certain age. There is a reasonably priced and tasty menu with an Italian slant. Walkers and dogs are welcome. Seven real ales are available, with constantly changing guests and it is planned to re-open the pub's own brewery in the adjacent building.

Open every day from 12 noon.
☎ *01430 873 849; www.goodmanhamarms.co.uk*

East Yorkshire

1 From the **Goodmanham Arms**, turn right and walk uphill. When you pass the church, turn immediately left, opposite **Rectory Farm**. At the end of the road, continue in the same roughly northerly direction along a track which passes beneath an old railway bridge. The track goes gradually uphill and bears left.

2 At a path junction just before the brow of the hill, continue straight ahead following the blue bridleway signs. About 50 yards

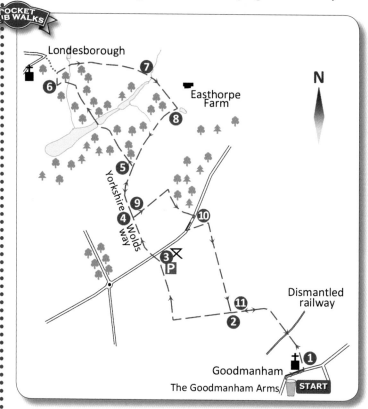

further on, another path goes off to the right. Keep straight on towards the top of the hill following the **Yorkshire Wolds Way** white acorn sign. The Yorkshire Wolds Way then turns sharp right round the edge of a field, still bearing gently uphill towards a main road in the distance.

Looking across to your left, you will have good views across the Vale of York and should be able to make out the distinctive wooded hill at Holme-on-Spalding-Moor and the cooling towers of distant power stations beyond.

3 Just before you reach the main road at **Towthorpe Corner** you will pass a lay-by with a small picnic site in a wooded area ahead and to your left. When you emerge onto the main road, cross with caution and continue in the same northerly direction alongside a hedge on your left. **Londesborough Hall** now comes into view in the woods ahead.

4 At the end of the first field there is a path junction. *If you are walking the shorter route, turn right here towards a plantation and*

Along the way

follow the instructions from point 9 below. Otherwise continue along the **Yorkshire Wolds Way**, now a surfaced track, in the same northerly direction towards Londesborough.

5 At the next path junction, turn left through a kissing-gate to follow the Yorkshire Wolds Way downhill into **Londesborough Park**. A large red-brick structure with arches known as the deer shelter comes into view up to the left, as well as the house nestling in trees ahead and to the right. As you approach the lake, bear slightly left. Go through a kissing-gate, cross the bridge and go through the next kissing-gate. Continue in a northerly direction over a slight rise, downhill to a metal gate and kissing-gate and then continue on the stony track bearing slightly to the left.

6 At the next junction go sharp right on the **Yorkshire Wolds Way**, signposted to Londesborough. Just before you reach the next kissing-gate turn right. There is a faint public footpath waymark.

Do not continue on the Wolds Way unless you wish to detour. Take the footpath to the right and follow the left-hand edge of the park in an easterly direction. Pass through two kissing-gates at the bottom of the slope. Continue up to the top of the hill in the same direction. The route is not evident on the ground; it goes up through rough pasture towards two trees at the top of the slope, from where you can see the next kissing-gate slightly downhill. Go through this kissing-gate and continue downhill between two large trees towards a stream at the bottom.

7 When you reach the stream, go through a kissing-gate, over the bridge and through the next kissing-gate. Carry straight on with a farm building up to your left – there is still no perceptible path. Bear down towards the dip on your right and you will see a wooden gate ahead about 20 yards up from the bottom of the dip.

Goodmanham **Walk 8**

8 Pass through the kissing-gate and turn right onto the **Easthorpe** farm track. Continue on this track in a south-westerly direction for ½ mile passing the entrance to **Londesborough Park** on your right (point 5). Retrace your steps for a short distance on the Wolds Way to the path junction at point 4.

9 At the path junction, turn up towards the plantation. It is not clear which side of the hedge you should walk. Either side will bring you out at the top of the field. Turn right at the top of the field and walk along the edge of the wood in a south-easterly direction until you reach the main road.

10 Turn right and walk down the verge for about 50 yards until you see the public footpath sign on the other side of the road. Cross with care and follow the field edge path going uphill with the hedge to your right. As the path levels out about halfway up the field, look out for a waymarked gap to your right. Pass through then continue down the left-hand side of a hedge. Ahead and to your left the church tower and village of **Goodmanham** come into view.

11 At the bottom of the field, rejoin the **Wolds Way** and turn left towards the village. When you reach the main road, turn right to return to the **Goodmanham Arms**.

Place of interest nearby

Londesborough, 4 miles north-west of Goodmanham, reached via Market Weighton, has an information board about the original Londesborough Hall which once stood here. Public footpaths run through the grounds and past the lake of the demolished house.

9 Beverley

The Woolpack Inn

(Photo courtesy of Rob Byass)

Beverley is a busy market town and is the historic county town of East Yorkshire. It has not one but two magnificent Gothic churches, the Minster at the southern end of the town and St Mary's church near the North Bar, the one remaining medieval gateway to the town. The town is fortunate in having several extensive commons. To the west is the Westwood, frequented

Distance – 3½ miles.

OS Explorer 293 Kingston upon Hull & Beverley GR TA028395.

Several ups and downs on firm, grassy terrain, with strategically-placed seats along the way.

Starting point The Woolpack Inn, Beverley HU17 8EN.

How to get there *Beverley is approximately 10 miles north of Hull. The Woolpack is located at 37 Westwood Road, a quiet residential street on the western edge of the town. Follow the one-way system, turn left off Lairgate into Grayburn Lane, then right onto Albert Terrace and left at the next junction into Westwood Road. The pub is on the left-hand side. Parking is restricted near the pub but is available on roadside verges at the top of Westwood Road on the route of the walk.*

by walkers, golfers and horse-riders alongside peacefully grazing cattle. It is designated Access Land where walkers are free to roam. It adjoins the Hurn, the site of Beverley racecourse.

The walk takes you up to the historic Black Mill, then climbs further up to the ancient woodland of Burton Bushes, particularly lovely in late spring when bluebells are in bloom. It affords splendid views back to the town with the towers of the Minster soaring above the trees on the skyline.

THE PUB There are dozens of pubs in Beverley, but the **Woolpack Inn** has a special charm. The quaint building dates back almost 200 years and consists of two former cottages with cosy rooms and log fires. The menu offers classic pub food augmented by daily specials.

Opening times are 4.30 pm to 11 pm on Monday to Tuesday; 12 noon to 2.30 pm and 4.30 pm to 11 pm on Wednesday and Thursday; 12 noon to 2.30 pm and 4.30 pm to 11.30 pm on Friday; 12 noon to 11.30 pm on Saturday; and 12 noon to 11 pm on Sunday. ☎ *01482 867095; www.thewoolpackbeverley.co.uk*

1 Turn left out of the pub and walk up to the top of **Westwood Road** until you reach the **Westwood pastures** with a gatehouse on your left. Pass through a kissing-gate on the right and take a faint grass track towards the little wood. Bear left, picking up a track in a slight dip heading for **Black Mill**. About halfway to the mill, cross over a wide gully (**The Gallop**). From here, a clear path heads a little to the left of the mill.

If you are ready for a pause, there are several memorial benches round the mill. Cattle also refresh themselves at the adjacent water trough. From here you can see the grandstand and white railings of the racecourse over to your right and, in the distance beyond, Nafferton Wold, possibly with a dusting of snow in winter.

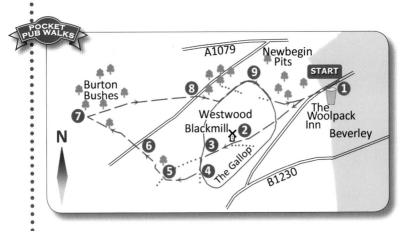

2 From **Black Mill**, pick up a green track, still leading in a westerly direction and heading towards the highest point on the horizon, a wooded hill with pylons to the left of it. Cross the fairway, checking for golfers who may be approaching from the left.

3 When you reach **The Gallop**, bear left and follow the path alongside it, passing a golfing green on your right. After passing the green and tee, cross the Gallop and continue for about 200 yards in the same direction. Then begin to bear diagonally right, skirting the gorse bushes on the slope to your right.

4 At the end of the bushes, bear downhill to the right into a sharp dip with a narrow path at the bottom. Then bear left towards the perimeter fence and pick up a path going uphill alongside a fence and hedge. This path descends again, down a steep, sometimes muddy, slope and passes a kissing-gate in the fence on the left.

5 Carry on up the hill where a welcome bench awaits, with a good view back to Black Mill and over the nearby golfing green. Continue following the perimeter path. As you approach a minor road ahead, the single tower of the lovely **St Mary's church** comes into view on your right, nestling amongst trees. Further to the right, the two towers of **Beverley Minster** rise majestically above the town.

6 Cross the minor road and continue following the perimeter fence towards the left-hand edge of the ancient woodland ahead of you known as **Burton Bushes**. When you reach the wood, you will be at the highest point of the walk.

7 Turn right to follow the edge of the wood. When you reach its south-east corner, keep heading towards **St Mary's church tower**, then bear downhill into the dip on the right and pick up a winding green path leading towards the two Minster towers.

East Yorkshire

[8] When you reach the minor road, cross over and pass between two golfing greens. Continue along a grassy track then bear right up a small path through a gap in the bushes. When you are almost at the top of the hill, cross the fairway with **Black Mill** to your right and continue towards the town along the line of the **Gallop** parallel with the minor road.

Glorious bluebells in Burton Bushes

[9] Follow the **Gallop** as it bears away from the road to the right. When **Black Mill** is directly to your right, turn left, heading for the corner of the little wood on your left. Keeping to the right of the wood, continue towards a terrace of four large houses. Turn right onto the path in front of them which leads you back to **Westwood Road**.

Place of interest nearby

The recently-built **Treasure House** in Beverley contains the art gallery, an upstairs café and a top-floor viewing area. Whilst in Beverley, you might also consider following one of the town trails which include an outdoor exhibition of paintings by the eminent Beverley-born artist Fred Elwell. Details of two town trails can be obtained from the Tourist Information Centre, in Butcher Row, close to Wednesday Market. ☎ 01482 391672.

The Crown & Anchor

This fine walk takes you northwards along the river floodbank to the peaceful upper reaches of the meandering River Hull, with wide views across the countryside. The route then skirts the lake at High Eske hidden amongst trees which may be unknown even to fairly local residents as it was not created until the late 1980s.

The lake and the adjacent Pulfin Bog Nature Reserve are rich in wildlife. There is an abundance of wild flowers along the lakeside path attracting many butterflies in summer. More than 100 different types of bird have been spotted in the area, including many migrant species.

Distance – 4 miles.

OS Explorer 293 Kingston upon Hull and Beverley
GR TA056417.

Good, level walking on grass and firm tracks.

Starting point The Crown & Anchor, Tickton HU17 9RY.

How to get there *Tickton is approximately 2 miles east of Beverley, just off the A1035 heading towards Hornsea and Bridlington. Hull Bridge is at the western end of the village. Some roadside parking is available close to Hull Bridge.*

THE
PUB

The **Crown & Anchor** has an attractive location on the east bank of the River Hull, with a sunny outdoor area along the riverside. It is a cheerful, busy spot with moored river boats and a campsite next to the car park. The friendly pub, with a family atmosphere, serves classic pub fare.

Opening times are from 12 noon, seven days a week. ☎ *01964 501854; www.marstonspubs.co.uk/crownandanchor-tickton*

1 From the front of the pub, descend to the adjacent bank of the **River Hull**, either using some rather steep stone steps in the corner of the pub forecourt or by using the ramp next to the footbridge. Turn right and go along the river, passing beneath the bridge carrying the busy road ahead.

2 Make your way up onto the floodbank and continue in a northerly direction alongside the river. After passing the polo ground on your right, cross over a stile. **Eske manor house** comes into view

just above the trees over to your right, and you will see a bumpy field, the site of the deserted village of **Eske**. After crossing over another stile, continue for 100 yards.

3 When the river on your left bears sharply to the left (in approximately 1¼ miles), leave the floodbank at a fork and take the waymarked footpath to the left. The route now continues between the river bank on your left and the lake which will now come into view on your right. Continue round the lake in a clockwise direction. You will pass the entrance to the **Pulfin Bog Nature Reserve** on your left where information boards are provided.

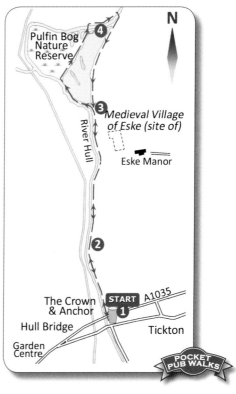

4 Eventually you will reach a footbridge and the **River Hull** once again comes into view on your left. Pass through a kissing-gate. From here, you can turn left to follow the river bank further north if you wish to extend your walk. Otherwise turn right to return to **Hull Bridge** on the well-used route along the floodbank. As you return, you will have fine views of **Beverley Minster** in the distance.

The River Hull

Place of interest nearby

The **Pulfin Bog Nature Reserve** passed on the route is rich in wildlife and well worth a visit. Visit the Yorkshire Wildlife Trust for more information: www.ywt.org.uk/reserves/pulfin-bog-nature-reserve

11 **Great Hatfield**

The Wrygarth Inn

This is probably one of the least well-known parts of East Yorkshire but has a fascinating history. At the end of the last Ice Age, when the ice retreated in about 8,500 BC, the landscape left behind is said to have resembled the Norfolk Broads with small hills, bogs, meres and hollows. The largest remaining mere or lake is Hornsea Mere – a lasting reminder of pre-historic times. The first two miles of the route follows the Hornsea Rail Trail, a multi-user trail which forms part of the Trans Pennine Trail (TPT) which runs across England from Hornsea to Liverpool.

Distance – 6 miles.

OS Explorer 295 Bridlington, Driffield & Hornsea and 293 Kingston upon Hull & Beverley GR TA183430.

Level walking, with a firm surface on the rail trail, followed by field paths and rough pasture.

Starting point The Wrygarth Inn, Great Hatfield HU11 4UY.

How to get there *Great Hatfield is approximately 3 miles south-west of Hornsea and can be reached by taking the B1242 from Hornsea to Mappleton then turning right onto a narrow country road for approximately 2 miles. The Wrygarth Inn is situated at the T-junction on the western outskirts of Great Hatfield and has a car park to the rear. Cars can also be parked on wide verges near the access to the rail trail at point 10 of the walk.*

THE PUB The Wrygarth Inn is a family-friendly establishment and has a comfortable interior which includes a dedicated indoor play area for children just off the main dining room. Outside, there is a nine-hole crazy golf course and beer garden. The pub also houses the village sweet shop! Food is served in the roomy bar areas, as well as in the separate dining and carvery area. There is a comprehensive à la carte menu and good-value roast dinners are served every day.

In the summer, opening times are all day every day except Tuesday when it is closed. In winter, the pub is open from 12 noon to 2 pm and from 5 pm to 11 pm on Monday, Wednesday, Thursday and Friday; closed Tuesday; open all day on Saturday and Sunday. ☎ *01964 533300; http://wrygarthinn.co.uk*

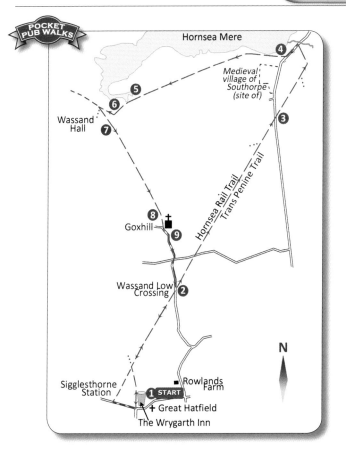

POCKET PUB WALKS

Hornsea Mere

④

Medieval
village of
Southorpe
(site of)

⑤

⑥

Wassand
Hall
⑦

③

Hornsea Rail Trail
Trans Pennine Trail

⑧ †
■
Goxhill
⑨

Wassand Low
Crossing ②

N

Sigglesthorne
Station

① START
■ Rowlands
Farm

† Great Hatfield

The Wrygarth Inn

1 From the front of the pub, turn immediately right and take the very narrow footpath signposted between a fence and a hedge alongside the pub car park. Keep on the narrow path along a wire fence to the end of the first field, then bear left through a wooden fence and turn right onto the old railway track.

2 After ¾ mile, the trail crosses a minor road at **Wassand Low Crossing**. About 400 yards further on, it crosses over another minor road at Goxhill crossing. Now continue for almost another mile until a red-brick road bridge comes into sight over the track. There are one or two benches along the track if you wish to pause.

3 Carry on under the bridge until the trail reaches the outskirts of **Hornsea**. Turn left at the end of the trail and take the path down through the allotments. When this path emerges onto a road, turn left. Cross over and walk along past the houses until you reach the first field on the right.

4 Turn right onto the footpath. At this point, **Hornsea Mere** comes into view. Bear to the left slightly diagonally across the field along a well-trodden green path. Grassy lumps and bumps are the remains of the medieval village of **Southorpe**. At the end of the field, pass through a fence and alongside a wire fence to your left, with the mere still visible on the right. At the end of the second field, go through a wooden kissing-gate and continue in the same westerly direction through three more fields on a well-trodden path keeping to the right of the hedge.

5 You will then reach a wooden kissing-gate with a 'Bull in Field' notice. This need not deter you as I have never actually seen a bull in this field, but should there ever be one, one is advised not to come between the bull and the cows. The route continues ahead on a clear grass track towards another gate. Pass through and continue towards the woods ahead. After a third kissing-gate, bear right over a wooden footbridge, then continue on the track diagonally across the next field.

6 You will now emerge through a kissing-gate onto a wide bridleway. Turn immediately right and pass through yet another kissing-gate. Follow the bridleway alongside the wood on your right towards a belt of trees ahead. As you approach the trees, look out for a

path going diagonally back across the field sharply to your left and follow it to a kissing-gate in the hedge.

If you continue on the bridleway for 100 yards beyond the narrow belt of trees, you will have an excellent view through a gap in the trees of Wassand Hall in parkland up to your left and of Hornsea Mere over to your right. Retrace your steps to rejoin the route and take the diagonal cross-field path which will now be to your right.

7. Pass through the kissing-gate and continue over very rough pasture in the same diagonal direction. Head for a wooden kissing-gate in the opposite hedge about 20 yards down from the top of the field. Continue diagonally across another two fields until you emerge near the hamlet of **Goxhill**.

8. Continue along a sometimes rather muddy track, then bear diagonally right, taking a faint path across a small field up towards **Goxhill church** in the trees ahead. The waymarked path passes through a gap just to the right of the church, keeping the farm buildings to your right.

9. At the front of the church, turn left onto the road. Soon you will reach a crossroads. Go straight ahead and continue until the road meets the railway track at **Wassand Low** crossing (2). Turn right onto the track and retrace your steps for ¾ mile along the track. Shortly after passing farm buildings over to the left, look out for the footpath on the left leading back to the **Wrygarth Inn**.

Place of interest nearby

Hornsea museum in the seaside resort of Hornsea, 4 miles north-east of Great Hatfield, is well worth a visit. It reflects the changing patterns of village life in North Holderness over the past centuries. ☎ 01962 533443.

The Dog & Duck

This attractive walk takes you through a pleasant, former deer park to the south of the village, then along undulating paths and tracks climbing gently towards Risby, the site of a great house where Henry VIII was once entertained. A short detour off the main route takes you down to a peaceful, secluded lake.

Distance – 5¾ miles.

OS Explorer 293 Kingston upon Hull & Beverley GR SE996372.

Well-trodden paths, tracks and roadside verges.

Starting point The Dog & Duck, Walkington, HU17 8SX.

How to get there *Walkington is situated approximately 2 miles south-west of Beverley on the B1230 road to South Cave. The Dog and Duck is situated on the main street of the village, on the corner of Northgate. For those not visiting the pub, alternative parking is available on the route of the walk near Walkington church on Little Weighton Road.*

THE PUB The quaint exterior of the **Dog & Duck** belies its open-plan, recently refurbished interior, where you will find a pleasant and spacious dining area and a menu with enough variety to suit most tastes and pockets. There is a large parking area and a few outdoor tables to the rear with a new beer garden planned. Food is served throughout the day.

Opening times are from 11.30 am on Monday to Saturday and from midday on Sunday. ☎ *01482 881622*

1 To start the walk, cross over the often busy main street and head southwards up narrow **Kirk Lane**, almost immediately opposite. At the top of the lane, turn left onto **Little Weighton Road** towards the church. At the end of the road, continue in the same direction on a gravelled path alongside the cemetery.

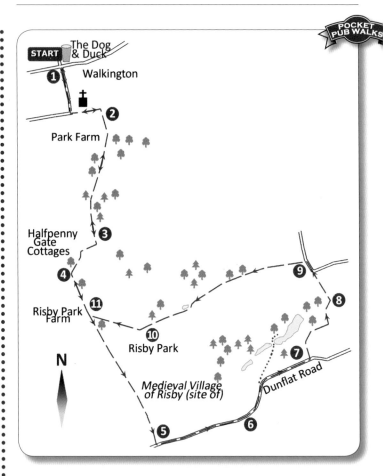

2 At the end of the first field, turn right onto a footpath which takes you past farm buildings and through a kissing-gate. At the end of the next field, go past a redundant stile and follow the waymarked route indicated by white posts across a meadow. The route bears

slightly to the right, leading towards the right-hand corner of a small wood ahead. Skirt round the wood on your left passing another redundant stile and take the faint path ahead and slightly to the right. This leads uphill towards a metal gate.

3 Pass through the kissing-gate beside it and turn right onto a wide track. The track bears left then right passing a bungalow on your right (**Halfpenny Gate Cottages**) and meets a surfaced farm track.

4 Turn left onto the track (waymarked 'Beverley 20') which leads to **Risby Park Farm** on your right. Continue straight ahead, going gently uphill for a good ½ mile until you reach the minor road known as **Dunflat Road**.

5 Go through the small wooden gate to the side of the metal gate and turn left onto the road which has a wide grass verge on the opposite side allowing for safe walking. Before reaching the brow of the hill, it is worth crossing over to read the information board situated on the fence of the last field before the farm buildings on your left.

Across the fields on the left you can clearly see grassy terraces, remnants of the deserted village of Risby and the grand house which once stood there. It was here that Sir Ralph Ellerker, then owner of the house and deer park, entertained his royal visitor, Henry VIII, in 1540. The last house on the site was demolished after a fire.

6 Continue towards the brow of the hill, passing **Park Farm** on your left. As the road begins to level out, you will pass the track down to **Risby Park** fishing ponds where the Folly Lake café, with a deck overlooking the water, is open to the public when fishing is in progress. It is worth a detour to visit the lake. Then continue along the road passing **Folly Wood** on your left.

[7] At the end of the wood, turn left onto a narrow footpath waymarked 'Beverley Beaver Trail'. Follow this path alongside the wood where bluebells abound in late spring. Do not enter the wood ahead, but keep to the footpath which bears right then left as it skirts round it.

In school summer holidays, a maize maze and other attractions for children are usually set up in the field to your right (accessible from Dunflat Road).

[8] Keep bearing to the left round the wood until the path descends into a dip. Cross over and continue up into the field beyond. The path leads up between two fields. The right of way then passes

The tranquil Folly Lake near the route of the walk

through a gap in the hedge to your right and emerges onto a fairly busy road. Follow the road for about 50 yards, using the left-hand verge.

9 Turn back into the field on a wide track signposted on the left-hand side of the road. Continue straight ahead on this track which then bears right towards the field edge, down into a dip then up towards a wood. Skirt round the left-hand side of the wood.

10 At the bottom of the hill, look for a waymarked path which leads diagonally ahead and to your right up a sloping field. If this path is impassable, an alternative green track is available along the outside to the left of the field.

11 When you emerge at the top of the rise, turn right onto the surfaced track passing **Risby Park Farm**. Bear right, then left and right again, past a bungalow. You will shortly reach a kissing-gate into the field on your left. Keep to the left-hand side of the field, passing under a large beech tree, then bear right to skirt round the wood on your right. At the end of the meadow, pass through a kissing-gate and retrace your steps to **Walkington** on the footpath. Turn left at the end, go past the church and turn right down **Kirk Lane** into the village centre.

Place of interest nearby

A visit to the nearby market town of **Beverley**, with its rich cultural history and quaint medieval buildings is highly recommended. The 600-year-old Dominican Friary building near the Minster is an outstanding example of medieval architecture, restored and brought back to life as a youth hostel.

13 **Skidby**

The Half Moon

This walk from the attractive village of Skidby will reward you with some impressively wide views towards the plain of Holderness in the east, the distant skyline of Hull to the south and the towers of Beverley Minster to the north. In late spring, a short diversion offers the magical sight of a bluebell wood. The village boasts Yorkshire's only working windmill which operates at weekends, weather permitting.

Distance – 3 or 4½ miles.

OS Explorer 293 Kingston upon Hull & Beverley GR TA018337.

Mainly gently undulating field paths.

Starting Point *The Half Moon, Skidby HU16 5TG.*

How to get there *Skidby is just off the A164 between Hull and Beverley. The Half Moon is situated in Main Street at the eastern end of the village. For those not patronising the pub, street parking is available on the minor road near Skidby Mill.*

THE PUB

The **Half Moon** welcomes walkers and serves traditional bar meals, as well as the 'man-sized' filled Yorkshire puddings for which it is renowned. The pub was built over 350 years ago, reputedly using bricks from Hull's ancient city wall.

It is open from 12 noon to 11 pm Sunday to Thursday and from 12 noon to midnight on Friday and Saturday. ☎ 01482 643403

1 On leaving the **Half Moon** car park, turn right into **Main Street** and walk down through the village. Notice on the way some good examples of East Yorkshire herringbone brickwork on the gable ends of the farm opposite number 37 and also on the house at 55 Main Street.

2 Opposite the church, turn right into **Church Rise**. When the road bears right, continue straight ahead through a metal gate and then on a path through pasture which passes through low trees on either side. Notice the remains of an old chalk quarry ahead and to the right. On emerging from the trees, the path bears diagonally right and crosses a chalk track. Enter the woodland ahead through

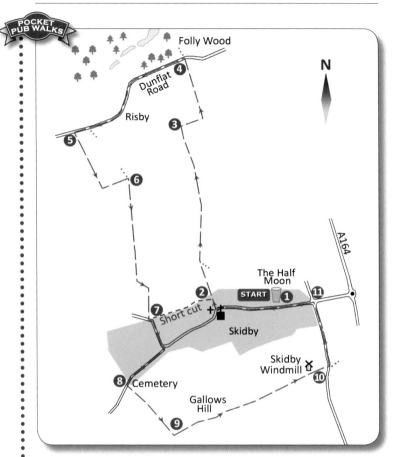

a metal gate below and to the right of the chalk track and take a parallel waymarked bridleway which leads up through a pretty, wooded ravine known as **Oldgate**. At the top of the ravine turn left and go up into a field. Turn immediately right onto the track which continues in a mainly northerly direction, eventually with open views to your right.

3 Turn right following the field edge with views of Beverley Minster ahead and also of the distant Hull skyline. At the corner of the field, the track turns left and emerges on to a minor road known as **Dunflat Road**.

In late spring, you may wish to divert from the main route at this point and enter Folly Wood by a path across the road. A little way down this path where it begins to bear right, bluebells grow in profusion in the woods ahead.

4 Turn left along the minor road and pass the entrance to the **Folly Lake** fish ponds on your right. (Refreshments are usually available in the lakeside café here at weekends.) Continue on past a farmhouse. Shortly after the farm track, you will be able to discern some earthed-over terracing to the right, once the site of a former manor house. Just before the end of the first field after the farm track, a display board on the right tells us that in 1540, the house and deer park belonged to Sir Ralph Ellerker and that he once entertained King Henry VIII here.

5 Opposite the display board, turn left onto the field-edge path indicated by a finger-post. At the top of the field, the path bears left then, about halfway up the field, look out for a gap in the hedgerow on your right.

6 Turn right through the gap and follow a clear path leading towards pylons. Bear left at a pylon, then right again to join the road on the outskirts of **Skidby village**.

7 *(When the track emerges onto Little Weighton Road there is an optional shortcut back to the pub. Take the narrow, waymarked footpath which passes behind the houses almost immediately to your left. This will bring you back to Church Rise).* The longer route takes you down the road ahead. At the T-junction, turn right into **Riplingham Road**. Continue to the last house on the left.

8 After passing a small cemetery, turn left onto the track marked by a fingerpost. Follow this track steadily uphill keeping to the left of the hedge. **Skidby windmill** now comes into sight across the field to your left.

9 At a junction of three paths, turn left up **Gallows Hill** towards the mill. Ahead and to the right you will again have panoramic views of the Hull skyline. As you get closer to the mill, the distant towers of the Humber Bridge eventually come into sight behind and to your right.

10 Near the mill, pass through a kissing-gate with a paddock to your right. Turn left at the end of the paddock.

You may wish to pause here to visit Skidby Mill and the Museum of East Riding Rural Life (entrance on your left). Flour from the mill is on sale in the museum shop.

To continue back to the start, bear right past the side of the **Millhouse restaurant** until you reach the main road. Turn left at the road and continue to the crossroads.

11 Turn left into **Main Street** and after a short distance you will reach the **Half Moon pub** on your right.

Place of interest nearby

Skidby Windmill, on the south-western outskirts of the village was built in 1821 and is Yorkshire's last working windmill. Weather permitting, its sails turn every weekend and it continues to produce its own wholemeal flour (on sale on the premises) from locally-grown wheat. The building houses the Museum of East Riding Rural Life, together with a shop and toilet facilities. Further details including admission charges can be found at: www2.eastriding.gov.uk/leisure/museums-and-galleries/east-riding-museums-and-galleries

14 South Cave

The Fox & Coney

South Cave has an elegant town hall, with a distinctive clock
tower, and an impressive Gothic castle dating from 1787. This
was once a private residence but now operates as a hotel and
its grounds form the local golf club. The walk offers lovely views
across the Vale of York and the Humber estuary, and includes a
short part of the Yorkshire Wolds Way. Red kites can sometimes
be seen wheeling in the skies above the hills.

Distance – 3 miles.

OS Explorer 294 Market Weighton & Yorkshire Wolds Central GR SE924315.

Two short, steep climbs.

Starting point The Fox and Coney, South Cave HU15 2AT.

How to get there *South Cave is on the A1034, approximately 7 miles south of Market Weighton, some 13 miles west of Hull and 12 miles south-west of Beverley. It can also be reached from the A63 junction, just north of Brough. The Fox & Coney is situated on the eastern side of the main road, just to the north of the staggered crossroads in the village centre. Parking is also available to the west of the crossroads on Church Road.*

THE PUB Originally built in 1739 as a coaching inn, the **Fox & Coney** has an attractive, recently-refurbished interior, with a paved beer garden and car parking to the rear. Food is served in the bar or in a separate restaurant area.

Opening times are 11.30 am to 11.30 pm every day. ☎ *01430 424044; www.foxandconey.co.uk*

[1] From the pub, turn left down the main road and then take the first street on the left, **Beverley Road**. Follow the road for about 400 yards until you see a fingerpost to **Brantingham** on the right-hand side. Take the track which becomes narrower as it leaves the village in an easterly direction. It passes through a plantation of coppiced trees, heading towards the hillside ahead. Ignore the faint track off to the left.

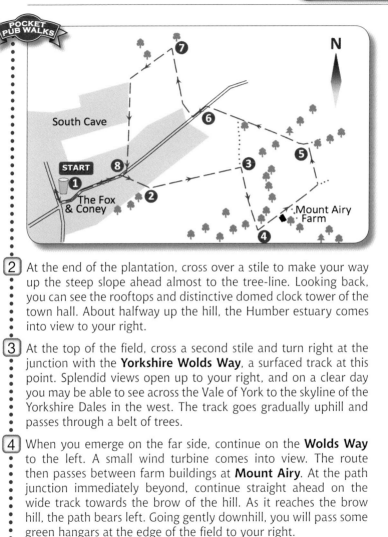

POCKET
PUB WALKS

South Cave

START

1

The Fox
& Coney

8

2

3

6

7

5

4

Mount Airy
Farm

N

2 At the end of the plantation, cross over a stile to make your way up the steep slope ahead almost to the tree-line. Looking back, you can see the rooftops and distinctive domed clock tower of the town hall. About halfway up the hill, the Humber estuary comes into view to your right.

3 At the top of the field, cross a second stile and turn right at the junction with the **Yorkshire Wolds Way**, a surfaced track at this point. Splendid views open up to your right, and on a clear day you may be able to see across the Vale of York to the skyline of the Yorkshire Dales in the west. The track goes gradually uphill and passes through a belt of trees.

4 When you emerge on the far side, continue on the **Wolds Way** to the left. A small wind turbine comes into view. The route then passes between farm buildings at **Mount Airy**. At the path junction immediately beyond, continue straight ahead on the wide track towards the brow of the hill. As it reaches the brow hill, the path bears left. Going gently downhill, you will pass some green hangars at the edge of the field to your right.

East Yorkshire

5 At the next T-junction, bear left down towards the trees in a north-westerly direction. A narrow, sometimes slippery, path continues down through the trees. At the bottom edge of the wood, it emerges onto a metalled farm road where you continue downhill to a road junction.

6 Turn left along the main road for a short distance. Cross over just before the new house on the right where there is a signpost indicating the Wolds Way route to North Newbald.

(At this point, you can follow the road all the way back to South Cave if you wish.)

Otherwise, to continue the walk, turn off to the right on the footpath alongside the garden. After about 100 yards, cross over a footbridge and ascend the hill with open views to the right.

7 When you reach the T-junction at the top, turn left onto the track. There will now be views on your left across to Lincolnshire on the south bank of the Humber. Continue downhill on this track which eventually bears left and joins a residential street. At the road junction, continue along the road in the same southerly direction, with a small stream in front of the houses on the right-hand side.

8 At the end of the road, turn right at the T-junction and follow **Beverley Road** for 400 yards to return to the main street. Turn right up the main street back to the **Fox & Coney**.

Places of interest nearby

North Cave, 2 miles west of South Cave, has a fine village church and on the outskirts of the village is the **North Cave Wetlands Nature Reserve** which is well worth a visit; www.northcavewetlands.co.uk

The Green Dragon

This lovely walk passes the old mill and the springs which feed the mill pond, then meanders along the bottom of delightful, steep-sided Welton Dale following the route of the Yorkshire Wolds Way. After a gentle climb to the head of the dale, the route continues through woodland, then returns along the side of Elloughton Dale, with excellent views of the Humber estuary and beyond.

East Yorkshire

Distance – 4½ miles.

OS Explorer 293 Kingston upon Hull & Beverley GR SE924315

Woodland paths, with one gentle ascent.

Starting point The Green Dragon, Welton HU15 1NB.

How to get there Welton lies just north of the A63, midway between South Cave and the Humber Bridge, and approximately 12 miles west of Hull. The Green Dragon can be found close to the duck pond and church. For those not visiting the pub, there is a car park at the southern end of the village near the A63 footbridge.

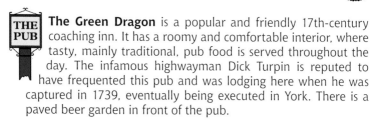

THE PUB **The Green Dragon** is a popular and friendly 17th-century coaching inn. It has a roomy and comfortable interior, where tasty, mainly traditional, pub food is served throughout the day. The infamous highwayman Dick Turpin is reputed to have frequented this pub and was lodging here when he was captured in 1739, eventually being executed in York. There is a paved beer garden in front of the pub.

Opening times are 11 am to 11 pm Monday to Thursday; 11 am to 11.30 pm Friday and Saturday and 12 noon to 11 pm on Sunday.
☎ *01482 666700; www.greendragonpubwelton.co.uk*

1 From the front of the pub, go straight ahead passing the church and pond on your right. Go up as far as the five-way road junction and take the second road on the left, **Dale Road**. The old water mill comes into view over to the right. Continue past the pond on the right and enter **Welton Dale**.

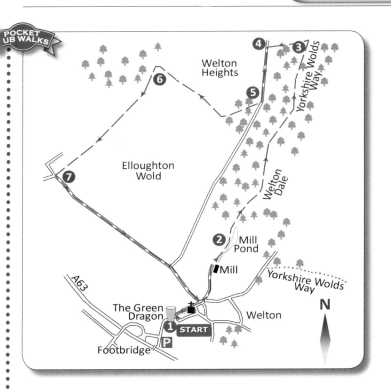

Welton
Heights

Yorkshire Wolds
Way

Welton
Heights

Elloughton
Wold

Welton
Dale

Mill
Pond

Mill

Yorkshire Wolds
Way

A63

The Green
Dragon

Welton

START

P

Footbridge

N

2 The track continues with ponds on either side. Bear right as it fizzles out at the last house, then go through a metal kissing-gate into the steep-sided dale. Follow the grassy track which meanders along the bottom. Continue winding your way gently uphill until you reach another metal kissing-gate. Pass through and continue on a well-defined path. This path narrows towards the top of the dale. Just before the top, at a metal gate, bear right and take the little path signposted **Wolds Way**.

3 At the head of the dale, when you emerge onto a surfaced track, cross over and turn left on the byway on the far side of

East Yorkshire

the fence which runs parallel to the track. At this point you leave the **Yorkshire Wolds Way** and are now following a route known as the **High Hunsley Circuit**. About halfway to the brow of the hill, you may be able to make out the shape of a large stone mausoleum in the trees over to your left.

4 When you reach the minor road at the top of the hill, cross over and turn left. Go gradually downhill along the road, passing the grounds of **Welton Heights** and a stable yard.

5 As the road bears right at the beginning of a wooded area to your right, look out for a yellow waymark and turn right through a kissing-gate onto a footpath through the wood. Follow the path through a wooded strip with fields on either side. The path re-enters woodland and reaches a footpath junction.

6 Turn left onto the path to **Elloughton**. Soon you emerge from the woods, with a magnificent view of the Humber estuary ahead of you. The path continues in a south-westerly direction along the left-hand side of the top of the dale. As you proceed along the dale, the path passes through a wooden kissing-gate and heads down towards the village of **Elloughton**.

7 When you reach the road junction at the bottom of the dale, turn left onto **Dale Road**. Go gradually uphill, still with views of the estuary to your right. At the next road junction, carry on straight ahead down **Kidd Lane**. At the bottom of the road, turn right to return to the village and the pub.

Place of interest nearby

The **Humber Bridge Country Park** local nature reserve at Hessle, approximately 6 miles to the east and accessible from the nearby A63, is a haven for wildlife, set amongst woods, meadows, ponds and cliffs.